CW00433033

I would like to dedicate this bool
John Cutland who was my proof
primary head teacher and author
he sifted his way through all the words and phrases within
and helped make it possible. Throughout his long life, he
passionately believed in the creative potential of young
people.

Liz Cutland

CONTENTS

Foreword

There was a meeting in 1977 that was not planned. It happened by chance. The meeting was between three people who discovered they had the same philosophy and a shared vision of improving the lives of young people. One of the three people was Dr. Howell Edwards.

Howell has played a key role in the development of Valleys Kids. It began because, as a Probation Officer, he listened to the young people he was working with and heard what they had to say. He started to work with them in groups that included, not just the clients, but their friends. This was not the norm. It was from those groups, meeting in a whitewashed coal cellar in1977, that Valleys Kids developed.

As a mentor, advisor, Board member and latterly as Chair, Howell's support has been fundamental as the organisation grew and developed.

It is very important that we not only listen to children, young people and families, but hear what they are saying. We have to encourage them to see their value and be part of the solution to the challenges in their lives and in the communities where they live. Over the past 35 years each development at Valleys Kids has been a response to their challenges and those of the communities in which they live.

We have been privileged to work with inspirational staff both paid and voluntary. They have shared our belief that everyone has value and that everyone matters. But the greatest privilege has been to see those children, young people and families, who have many challenges and disadvantages in their lives, begin to change, believe in themselves and achieve their potential. In reading this book you will hear some of their stories.

So we would like to thank all those people who have shared a belief in our work and supported the organisation. We are also very grateful to Liz for recording not only the journey of Valleys Kids but the effect it has on individuals and communities.

Read, enjoy, and believe that everyone has potential. Ensure that we not only listen and hear but act together to achieve positive change in people's lives.

Richard Morgan MBE and Margaret Jervis MBE DL
Co-founders of Valleys Kids

September 2013

Are You Listening?

'There are only two lasting bequests we can give our children: one is roots, the other is wings.'

This old Chinese proverb provides one of the main strands to this book.

The following tale has 3 closely related major themes that plait together, weaving their way through the pages and chapters of this document:

- A review of the history and maturation of a local charitable enterprise.
- An assessment of the value of helping to strengthen the roots and wings of young people
- An appraisal of the importance of improving and honing the art of listening to younger generations.

The primary thread follows the philosophy, growth and development of an organisation called Valleys Kids, which has the matter of community regeneration in its heart. Established in the Rhondda in South Wales in 1977, shortly before the closure of the collieries, its primary goal has been to help local communities help themselves to recover from this catastrophe.

As its name implies, the main attention of the organisation is centred on improving life for the young in the community. To this day, in all of the 4 neighbourhoods that have Valleys Kids centres embedded in the community, there are still large pockets of children living in poverty.

Poverty effectively silences people. So, the third interlaced ribbon of this account is about the special art of listening to communities that have been repressed. Hearing clearly what people in the neighbourhoods say has become a skill that Valleys Kids has refined over the years. The organisation has much to show us about paying attention to the voices of young people, particularly. Although there is much legislation in both the British and Welsh Governments about listening to children, this book argues that in general, we must make more of an effort if we genuinely want to hear what they have to say. That is, if we want to help them improve their lot in life and if we care about their future.

When combined with a sense of belonging, the provision of new experiences and the learning of new abilities, the skill of attentive listening is what lifts the expectations of those who have not dared to have aspirations before. That encouragement is what creates a feeling of connection, provides a sense of supportive community, strengthens the roots of our youth and raises their spirits, giving them the desire to stretch their wings and fly. In the following pages, many young people will talk of the experience of expanding their horizons.

This book will also demonstrate that although the South Wales valleys continue to have poor job prospects, Valleys Kids helps many young people find a pathway through to employment. This opportunity grows through voluntary work, different training courses and experience in the arts and music and ultimately through the discovery of special skills. Openings occur for many people, resulting from the improvement of self-esteem and the building of abilities that are central to Valleys Kids' ethos.

Living with poverty is a very personal experience. Through much investigation, I have discovered that it is rare to find a book on the regeneration of communities that comes from the point of view of the local people concerned. It is even more uncommon for the main voices of such a publication to come from the young. Although I express some personal opinions, my core intention has been to provide a vehicle so that the youngsters involved could use this book to tell their own story of growing up in Rhondda Cynon Taf, of their relationship with Valleys Kids over the years and of the new possibilities that are increasing for them as a result of this involvement.

A large part of my research has been participatory. I have spent time in all of Valleys Kids community projects: in Penyrenglyn, Penygraig, Pen Dinas and Rhydyfelin. More recently, I have been involved in the newer project in Porth. Although all of these neighbourhoods evolved from the development of the coal-mining industry, each has its uniqueness, its own individual history and characteristics. The changing faces of the communities are described through the eyes of the residents.

Among other activities, I have enjoyed taking part in away-days, in drama groups and in creative writing groups with young people. I have also sung in a community choir, participated in a musical extravaganza (along with several other artistic groups) in prestigious theatres in both Cardiff and Cape Town. I have interviewed 95 young people from Wales between the ages of 5 and 25, informally. My research also included 18 youngsters from South Africa.

All of these meetings were often in small groups of about 4 or 5 people. Occasionally, individuals chose to speak to me on their own.

I also contacted 45 adults who had experience of Valleys Kids. Some were 'kids' in the early days of the organisation. Others were family members who had received help in the past or were in receipt of support from the organisation at the time of writing this book. As before, I met with the grown-ups individually or in small groups. I spent time with a women's support group, Feeling Good Groups for each gender and a mixed art group. Additionally, I connected with a small number of mums from a Family Training group to learn about their involvement. I linked up with parents and children who jointly had experienced activities within the project. I got together with specialists from other agencies who work in partnership with Valleys Kids. I received much help from some of the professionals dedicated to encouraging young people who were discovering their potential through the arts in South Africa. I interviewed a further 24 adults who were either trustees of the charity or members of staff to hear matters from their perspective. I was given free access to all parts of the organisation. Over a 3-year period, I gathered information from over 200 people.

One of my initial anxieties in preparing for the research was that young people would not respond to an older person with obvious greying hair. My method was fairly laid back and I discovered that what worked best was an uncomplicated approach. I had 3 basic questions:

1. Why is this group/club/organisation important to you?
2. What has it done to help you?
3. What would make it better?

What I discovered very quickly was that people of all ages warmed to the title Can You Hear Me? and wanted to tell me their stories. I have been very moved by the generosity of their sharing. Obviously, with such personal experiences, confidentiality was an issue. I have been given permission to use most of their names. Some have asked that I give them a different name. Others, who chose to tell of their experience 'so that other people can understand', have asked to have their name removed. There were one or two whose experience was so painful that we decided together it was necessary to generalise the description and depersonalise it. Each person whose experience I pass on has seen what I have written about them and has been given the option to have it removed. Every request has been treated with respect and fulfilled accordingly.

I have investigated the archives of the organisation for historical facts. I have relied on some official statistics, drawing on these to give evidence of the effects of poverty and to widen the picture. I have also referred fairly extensively to the writings of experts in the different fields of working with people. However, the main messages that come through these pages are from the young people and families in some of the South Wales valleys.

There are far too many contributors to name but I am very grateful to all those people who gave me so much of their time and experience and helped make this book possible. I include those who shared their stories, those who donated their poems, photographs and artwork, along with those who did all the practical stuff which was needed to put this book together and those who kept encouraging me when I needed it.

I hope you hear what they have to tell us. They have much to teach us, I believe.

PART ONE

The Resonance
of History

CHAPTER 1

Voices from the Past

'My first recollection of my birthplace is of mountains, not trees, but black mountains, dusty, dirty, and grey to the look and feel, everything monochrome, no green, and no bright warm colours, nothing to warm the soul. Dirt was everywhere, in the house, on the roof, ingrained and etched into the faces of people. Black and white, white and black, grey and grey, dark and dark, dust and dust ... this was the Valley into which I was born.'

As written by Roy Tomkinson in Of Boys, Men & Mountains.

This is one man's description of his experience of growing up in the Rhondda in the 1950s. It also portrays the environmental greyness of the world from which Valleys Kids was founded around a quarter of a century later: a period just before the coalmines were coming to an end.

As mentioned in the introduction to this book, Valleys Kids started as a small organisation in Penygraig, near Tonypandy in 1977 in Rhondda Fawr in the South Wales Valleys less than 20 miles north of Cardiff. At that time it was called the Penygraig Basement Project, officially.

However, local people referred to the centre as the Bike Club and they still do to this day for reasons explained in the next chapter. It is a registered charity, which has community regeneration in its heart and works with children and their families, helping them to help themselves. Listening to what they have to say. Encouraging them to discover their own innate potential to improve their lot in life.

Before we learn more about the growth, ethos and workings of that organisation it is necessary to have some understanding of the background in which Valleys Kids is rooted. It is impossible to appreciate its work for over 30 years in communities of Rhondda Cynon Taf without first exploring the geographical and historical implications, as well as the socio economic influences: examining their effect on the young people growing up in this area. Events of the 19th and 20th centuries left behind a huge and complicated legacy. The valleys are still in the long process of recovery from the impact of those times. A progressing period of social recession and deprivation followed the closure of the collieries, alongside a deep and continuing financial depression.

It is unrealistic to try and listen to the thoughts and feelings of local and modern young people without consulting the voices of the past and hearing their profound influence on what is happening today. The history of the South Wales valleys has not been kind to the majority of children who grew up here in years gone by. Yet, many have turned this challenging experience around. What the hardship through the years has highlighted is the courage and resourcefulness of the people of this region, their ability to survive tough conditions and to adapt to powerful changes. That independent spirit has to be acknowledged: to be respected and celebrated.

HISTORICAL LEGACIES

Although there are no longer any active mines in this area, we cannot talk about it without mentioning the word coal and its pervasive and conflicting effects on the community. According to Barbara Freese who wrote a book entitled Coal - A Human History, *'It triggered the industrial revolution, became the most powerful force on the planet, and created an industrial society the likes of which the world had never seen.'* This rapidly changing world became dependent on coal for energy - for transport, for the running of industries, for warmth, for comfort. It helped humanity transform nature's cold into something more attractive, and more civilised. In the 19th century the Rhondda had over 60 mines producing good quality coal. This contributed hugely to the British economy. Picture the pride of the valleys' residents in being in the forefront of this wave of change, of being needed so much: but also be aware of what they had to do for it, what they had to risk and sacrifice. Coal offered work to many; it allowed some families to raise their standard of living. Agricultural workers rushed to the minefields for employment.

It was a hard way of existing. For meagre wages, men risked life and limb to provide for their dependents. There being no minimum wage policy in place, how much was earned was dependent on how much coal was excavated. At times women were expected to work in the pits too. Throughout the years, the women's role was to hold the family together, making sure that the men had enough to eat so that they had the energy to tackle hard and exhausting work. To help supplement the family income, children sometimes younger than 8 were expected to work in these dangerous conditions, also putting their lives in jeopardy.

The feeling of fear must have been a constant companion for the majority of young people who worked deep in the bowels of the earth.

Disregard for the safety of children weaves its way through the history of coal mining. Today, Valleys Kids runs a community project in a neighbourhood called Pen Dinas. This is built close to the pithead of the first mine in the Rhondda, sunk in 1839. Noted in the Welsh Coal Mines web page, the very first recorded colliery explosion in the Rhondda was on New Years Day 1844, at this pit. Of the twelve people who were killed, 4 were boys. As in other industries, child labour was prevalent in those days.

BBC primary school history programmes researched the employment of working class children in Victorian Britain and considered the conditions of children working in the coalmines. It described them as dark, damp, dirty and dangerous with the only light coming from candles or oil lamps. Gas in the chambers could explode at anytime; tunnels could flood or collapse. Some children pushed trucks of coal, crawling along narrow underground passages. Others, called trappers, opened and shut wooden doors to let air pass through the tunnels. In order to do this they had to sit alone for long hours in the dark with no one to talk to. The National Museum of Wales holds records of the Children in Coal Mines Report of 1842. Among other things it describes the conduct of some adults in the mines as harsh and cruel, roughly using children. The feeling of fear must have been a constant companion for the majority of young people who worked deep in the bowels of the earth.

Historical evidence would suggest that the prominence of not listening to adults, let alone children is carved deep in the experience of the South Wales valleys. Certainly, this knowledge from the past teaches us much about the devastating effects of not being heard, not being valued. In researching documents, in listening to experiences of the industrial revolution, what strikes home is the total lack of care for those working in the mines. It has cost people their health; their livelihoods and lives of loved ones. The expectation was that people of all ages would work long hours, putting themselves at risk for the benefit of the privileged few. For many years the South Wales valleys were alive with mining activities. Coal was sent from here via the port of Cardiff to different corners of the world. Yet, availability of workers was taken for granted. Employers did not appear to value lives. If someone was killed in a pit accident it was assumed that another desperate for work would replace him very quickly. The wealthy minority were very powerful as well as very rich, turning a deaf ear to the effects of the working conditions on the adults and children they employed.

More recent history illustrates that conditions did not improve much over time. Some of those interviewed for this book, in their 50s and 60s remember the fear of their childhood, the acute awareness that their father's employment was dangerous. They could still vividly remember exactly where they were when news of pit disasters broke and precisely how they felt. One example of this was the accident at the Cambrian Colliery in Clydach Vale in 1965 when an explosion ripped through the mine killing 31 men and injuring 15. In retrospect, we can too easily forget that tragedies like these also left a number of families fatherless and traumatised.

Over a hundred years after the explosion in Pen Dinas, in 1966, the village of Aberfan (near Merthyr Tydfil) suffered one of the worst disasters in Welsh history. Despite concerns being raised a few years earlier, a mine-waste tip which was heaped on top of the mountain slid down into the valley, destroying the village primary school, killing 144 people in the process. One hundred and sixteen of them were children. By this time the pits had been nationalised.

We can conclude that the state was as careless as the private pit owners in listening to the needs of children: and as negligent of their welfare. Communities never really recover from catastrophes of this degree. The effect of shock and grief swells out: deep, far and wide.

Supplies of coal began to diminish. In 1955 a programme of pit closures began, the main mass shutting down from 1985 after the defeat of the strike of 1984. The coalmines closed even more quickly than they opened. Hywel Francis reflects in his book History on our Side (Wales and the 1984-85 Miners Strike). *'The strike in Wales had therefore not just been about picketing. It had been about how people began to take control of their lives.'* The different strikes over the years were difficult passionate battles of people fighting to protect their livelihoods, families and communities. Citizens who were trying hard to continue to eke out a living, asserted themselves collectively, hoping to be heard. However, Margaret Thatcher's Conservative government with their free market policies clashed with the National Coal Board and turned a deaf ear to the needs of the miners and their families. The strikes failed, people returned to work but the pits very quickly continued to close, leaving communities overwhelmed and depressed with unemployment and large numbers of people leaving the area.

GEOGRAPHICAL INFLUENCES

The geography of the vicinity also has an effect on the communication of the people of the valleys. Before the mines took over this area this was a quiet rural spot. The discovery of coal had galvanised this countryside into something quite different. After less than 150 years, the disappearance of the mines was as rapid as the earlier process of urbanisation. In the aftershock of the closures,

Access to villages within the natural geographical boundaries is made relatively easy; towns in neighbouring valleys maybe seen as closer on the map but there is little connection between them because of the intervening mountains.

the region has struggled to redefine itself and find its way with a new identity; again.

Today, Valleys Kids' work with young people and their families is centred mainly in four different communities within the county borough of Rhondda Cynon Taf or RCT, as it is known locally. From north to south, these neighbourhoods are known as Penyrenglyn, Penygraig, Pen Dinas and Rhydyfelin. RCT is a relatively new county and was formed in 1996 by the merger of the former Mid Glamorgan districts of Rhondda, Cynon Valley and a large part of Taf-Ely, its name embracing all of these areas. The county borough borders Merthyr Tydfil and Caerphilly in the east, Cardiff and the Vale of Glamorgan to the south, Bridgend and Neath, Port Talbot the west and Powys to the north.

Although this area's reputation for good coal was international, people outside Wales seem unaware that there are 2 Rhondda Valleys – the Rhondda Fawr (large) and the Rhondda Fach (small), branching away at the town of Porth and then lying alongside each other with mountains in between. These two valleys are located roughly in the centre of a number of deep vales running parallel to each other, approximately going from north to south. They stretch across South Wales from Carmarthenshire in the west to Monmouthshire in the east. The physical shape of the Rhondda valleys has a containing yet confining effect on local culture. Those living at the top of each valley have more difficulty in being accessible. Roads stretch along their floors connecting the different settlements within the particular basins. Access to villages within the natural geographical boundaries is made relatively easy; towns in neighbouring valleys maybe seen as closer on the map but there is little connection between them because of the intervening mountains.

The South Wales Valleys provided Britain's only mountainous coalfield. As the coalmines developed, this landscape defined the shape of the mining communities. According to census reports, there were less than 1000 people living in the Rhondda in 1851, 17,000 by 1871, and 153,000 by 1911 - a sweeping change occurring within 60 years. However, the wider impact of urbanisation was constrained by geography and the Rhondda remained a collection of villages rather than a town in its own right. To the present day, there is no natural centre, no 'capital' or major town of the Rhondda Valleys, which raises questions about where it is 'anchored' and whether this might have an effect on the ease of communication, particularly with the outside world.

Cardiff, the capital city of Wales since 1955, once among the most important coal ports in the world, lies just to the south of the Rhondda. A lot of its past wealth, a number of its beautiful buildings result from the money created by the hazardously hard graft that happened in the valleys during the peak of the mining development. A relatively new capital, charged with the responsibility of an even newer devolved government it is growing in stature within the British Isles and the rest of the world. As a city it bustles, with modern buildings and shopping precincts springing up despite the recent recession. Some changes have happened within Rhondda Cynon Taf in recent years - new roads have been built, new schools and hospitals erected. However, when travelling south from the valleys to the M4 corridor and Cardiff, there is still a feeling of moving from one economy into another and a sense that the importance of the mining areas has been left behind somewhere in times past.

As an incomer to the Rhondda, a Scot living in Wales for the past 11 years, I think the present day valleys have a unique and distinctive beauty – not quite urban, not really rural, sort of a mixture of both. Rows of terraced houses run along the bottom of the valleys and then tier their way up the hills predominating the inhabited landscape. At the top of the mountains perch some sheep farms. It is a very green panorama; fields, moorland and woods cling to the steep hillsides. In places, historic coal tips rise higher than the real mountains but in the process of greening they have found a way to blend into the natural setting. The Rivers Taf and Rhondda once clogged with the debris from the mines are now reported to have salmon swimming there. Heron and kingfishers can be seen flying along their courses. Environmentally, life could be seen as having improved dramatically. However, boarded up houses, derelict chapels and social clubs, deserted places of past employment all remind us sharply of the depth of damage done to these communities and prompt us to acknowledge that the healing from those times is far from complete.

Many local people enjoy the valleys' return to their natural beauty; others, conditioned by the past have difficulty seeing or appreciating it. Children are no longer born into the monochromic atmosphere described in Roy Tomkinson's book. Yet, the iconic image of the local area is rooted in its history, in the blackness of coal dust. Visitors express their delighted surprise at the change but - the outside world still hangs on to the old industrial picture of this area. To outsiders, the Rhondda was once the best known of these valleys for producing coal and despite the well-publicised closure of the pits and the passing of time, it is that loud and conflicting voice of history that prevails today, still.

LINGERING CHALLENGES

While acknowledging the wonderful changes, it is perhaps best not to be too easily seduced by the attractiveness of the landscape and the fact that groups of people are no longer putting their lives at risk by working deep underground. Hidden in these valleys are still some deep, complex and inherited social problems. Even now, the greatest challenge is that there remain large pockets of children and their families living in poverty: three generations of unemployment, in some cases.

Although Wales was able to boast that family poverty fell faster here than in other parts of the UK in the first half of the last decade, it was noted in 2005 that roughly a third of the 170,000 Welsh children who lived below the poverty threshold were from the South Wales valleys. Approximately one third of British children live in poverty today. In the 1970s – the proportion was one in ten. According to a Save the Children report (January 2011) Wales has slipped back in its recovery and has now the highest proportion of children living in poverty of any country in the UK, much of it hidden. It states that, *'In the valleys and other parts of Wales where industry and manufacturing have shut down, poverty is deep and long-standing.'* Many of the young living in local areas do so in relative comfort but there are still large social closets in our valleys communities where families live well below the poverty line. There are people from the Rhondda who would argue that many of those living here never really had the experience of coming out of the last recessions (1980s and 1990s). The effect is that families have been devastated for years, with cumulative disadvantage seeping through the generations.

On top of all of this deprivation, the structure of many families changed. Leading up to the closure of the mines Dad, who had always been the breadwinner was on strike and then later unemployed, if he was a miner. In the 1970s, women's role altered during these dramatically changing times. A lot of the drive and energy for creating the strikes came from the women in the community. Eventually, it was mums who were more likely to find jobs (most of them part time), usually in factories. In turn, this meant men who had more time on their hands, were expected to play a different and more direct role with the children. The closure of the coalmines transformed the lives of those living here more than most outsiders can imagine.

Twenty-five years on, Rhondda Cynon Taff continues to struggle with a number of socio-economic problems that came in the wake of the closure of the mines. There has been very little alternative employment. Since then, a minimal amount of industry has moved into this area. The mountainous terrain with steep valley walls does not encourage the influx of new industrial initiatives. A large number of people commute to Cardiff or near the M4 corridor for work. There has been a large migration of the well - qualified to other parts of the United Kingdom, as well as abroad. Educational attainment for those that live here is recorded as low with a large proportion of people having few or no qualifications. Schools are struggling to improve their record. A high ratio of people report long-term health problems like cancer and mine-related respiratory illnesses. According to David L. Adamson and Meic Stephens in their book Living on the Edge. *'Limiting long term illness is evident in all age groups at higher rates than elsewhere in the UK.'*

One of the local council's responses to the housing problem in the 60s and 70s was to build large council estates sometimes high on the mountains with what are now beautiful views. This was intended to be a positive response to the deteriorating condition of some of the terraced housing. However, many of the families who came from all over the valley to the new homes had multiple problems (no income apart from state benefits, alongside poor housing, health and prospects). They moved in with no roots in the area, no infrastructure set up to support them. Envisage the isolating effect that had on families. Imagine the dividing off of the neighbourhood from the wider area. This lack of community identity transpired largely as a result of these housing policies, the consequences of which were not fully thought through. One of the greatest assets of living within the mining areas was the tradition of neighbourhood support through the tough times, of listening to each other's problems and working through them together. The best intention to provide new housing was undermined by not acknowledging that intrinsic need.

A 2009 BBC report by the Home Editor (Mark Easton's UK) highlights the fact that Rhondda Cynon Taff came second highest in a list of counties in England and Wales for the number of prescriptions of antidepressants per head of population. The writer concludes that there may be many complex reasons for this. However, we cannot ignore the undermining effect of social deprivation on the morale of the communities. The people of the Valleys have a long history of resourcefulness. For some that ability seems to have been stifled, buried under decades of not being heard; submerged under a feeling of powerlessness and great sense of loss.

There is a lingering sense of bereavement in this area amongst the older generations: a void that has not quite been filled again. In proportion, memories of problems like a history of heavy drinking and violence seem to have faded and are denied. Some pensiveness and sadness for losing a way of life remain which included a very close community support network. The miners' institutes alongside church or chapel often provided cohesion in the community. These institutes, owned by miners' groups, were often of a socialist and altruistic nature, more often than not containing small libraries and reading rooms. They were an attempt to allow the working class men to better themselves through education. As well as taking care of intellectual needs, they also catered for the social side of the community, providing such things as a billiards hall, a refreshment hall and a large hall, which could be used for entertainment. The workingmen's institutes were often regarded as the centre of the community. Sadly, the closure of the pits meant that miners could no longer afford to support them financially and a lot of the buildings have been left to ruin, taking that social heart with them.

Churches and chapels have suffered a similar demise. As the new population centres grew, the first half of the 19th century was a period of great passion and massive expansion for all nonconformist sects in Wales. Local people took up the challenge of creating their own places of worship, giving ordinary people a voice and a sense of involvement. Now, as with the rest of the United Kingdom, the church, both conformist and non-conformist has lost its influence on the greatest majority of the population. In South Wales, that decline has left behind even more empty derelict buildings. The gradual closure of once well-attended centres of worship brought the loss of yet another strut in the structure of community support.

Some of today's members of Valleys Kids men's groups who had been employed in the pits talked longingly about the old days. It did not appear to be the dangers of the work

'I could wander anywhere. My mother knew I would be looked after. All the women in my street were my aunties even though we had no blood ties. They kept an eye open for me and made sure I was safe.'

they missed but the binding camaraderie that grew from working together in dangerous conditions. Nothing has really replaced that. In the women's groups there was also a wistfulness and yearning for the old community networks. One woman described her childhood:

'I could wander anywhere. My mother knew I would be looked after. All the women in my street were my aunties even though we had no blood ties. They kept an eye open for me and made sure I was safe.' She concluded that degree of a neighbourhood sense of responsibility has disappeared in the majority of communities; that many of today's children do not benefit from this combined level of care. In times past, there was also a solidarity that came from everyone fighting to survive in the working class community: being poor together. Everyone was seen as equal in his or her plight.

In the present, adults in their 50s and 60s, attending the centres reflect on the fact that front doors were never locked – a different reality from today. Although there is an appreciation that some have been able to improve their lot, the level of trust has diminished as the feeling of inequality within the local neighbourhoods grew – as some found ways of moving on, while others remained stuck in their situation.

Some children currently living in poverty have parents and sometimes grandparents who suffered for many years the effects of growing up in a neighbourhood where there has been little hope. This sense of hopelessness can lay a mantle of depression over many of our communities that lasts for decades. If you have been excluded from social activities because you are perceived as different: if you have been told directly or indirectly that you are not good enough, that you are less than…you begin to believe

'While poverty is often seen in only economic terms, we believe there is also a poverty of spirit. To help people out of social deprivation and economic poverty you must first tackle the poverty of spirit...'

it. You absorb that judgement into your being and act accordingly – either with great anger and aggression or, most commonly with a great sense of defeat. Sue Gerhardt sums this up in her book The Selfish Society, *'In practice, poverty in affluent nations has less to do with extreme hunger, disease or lack of shelter, and more to do with psychological hopelessness.'*

The founders of Valleys Kids wrote in a report entitled Hidden Potential in 1996. *'While poverty is often seen in only economic terms, we believe there is also a poverty of spirit. To help people out of social deprivation and economic poverty you must first tackle the poverty of spirit...'*

The following pages will illustrate that that is what Valleys Kids has been doing for over 33 years – tackling the poverty of spirit, building on the resourcefulness of young people, their families and communities and encouraging the development of close, neighbourhood support networks. Listening to what people of all ages are saying, particularly children; helping them to formulate some dreams and to move forward to embrace them; assisting them to find the courage to change their lives for the better. All this is achieved by providing a network of professional friendship.

CHAPTER 2

Finding Answers

'I had always been told what to do. At the Bike Club, I was loaned this very expensive camera to take photographs with. I had never been trusted like that before. That trust really improved my self-esteem. I learned about the beauty of things. It was a good experience. I felt wonderful, felt grown up and responsible. It was where I found my voice.'

This quote came from Audrey, who was one of the original members of the Penygraig Basement Project, then aged 15 years. She is now a businesswoman in Penygraig and a Trustee of Valleys Kids.

As I interviewed people who had been involved in the early stages of the Penygraig Basement Project and its successor the Penygraig Community Project, this statement of Audrey's seemed to me to be one which captured the essence of what these ventures were all about. That describes the fundamental nature of the organisation which is dedicated to helping people feel better about themselves and devoted to encouraging them stretch to their fullest capacity.

Expressions such as 'felt welcomed'; 'relaxed atmosphere'; 'helped my self confidence'; 'like a second family'; and 'felt involved'; 'not judged' were all frequently used.

Audrey views that positive experience in her adolescence as an important stepping-stone into her adult life. It helped launch her belief in her own abilities and to recognise what was then her hidden potential.

RECEIVING YOU LOUD AND CLEAR

This chapter is the anchor of the rest of the book with all other sections branching out from here. It mirrors the history of the organisation of Valleys Kids. While remaining true to the communities they serve, all projects that have evolved from the original grew from the influence of the central core of the Penygraig Community Projects. Chapter 2 describes this anchor: its purpose, its development, its rapid growth and the values in which it is embedded.

As we reflect, others will describe their experiences and what it meant to them with just as much feeling as Audrey. While interviewing different individuals, I was impressed by how Valleys Kids and its forerunning organisations impacted on people's lives. Even when the contact was for only one or two years, evidence shows that it obviously met a need at this time. For many, the influence continued into later life. In my research, the following key words and phrases appeared quite often to describe the projects. They came in various interviews with different people. Expressions such as *'felt welcomed'; 'relaxed atmosphere'; 'helped my self confidence'; 'like a second family'; and 'felt involved'; 'not judged'* were all frequently used. The common thread of helping people feel they are important runs through the history and ethos of this organisation.

Judging by the response from the people I have met during this survey, this appears to be part of the answer: helping people feel that they have something to contribute. The reaction to the organisation illustrates that what was essential was a caring response to the young people in the community. So, what was the call or need?

All too often we tend to think of communities as contained within the lines on maps. In assuming this, what we neglect to recognise is that communities are actually about the interactions of the people who live between those outlines. In the 1970s and following decades, relationships in the valleys' towns were greatly affected by the running down and subsequent closure of the pits. Whole neighbourhoods were out of work. Not only did this plunge a lot of families into poverty for many years, friendships were lost as people moved away seeking employment. Families were in turmoil as roles changed. Dads who had been proud to be the main breadwinners found themselves at home looking after the children while some mums were able to find employment as seamstresses in clothes-making factories. The image of a miner is a tough macho one and this was seriously challenged when the unemployed men were challenged to adapt to a more domestic role. The expectation in most mining communities was that the woman was responsible for the child rearing. It was a time of huge change - of devastation, confusion and fear.

The call that was initially answered by the Penygraig Basement Project was to support children, young people and their families who had political and industrial decisions thrust upon them, throwing many into turmoil and poverty, changing their lives forever. Some would have had problems anyway; the majority found themselves in a situation where they had little control over the outcome; all were dealt a hard blow in life. The need was to support those who wanted it while they were adapting to crisis and change. Also, in keeping with the culture of the valleys, helping them find a way through together.

'Valleys Kids is a celebration of the achievements of individuals and communities who through trying different activities and having different experiences broaden their horizons and achieve their potential.'

The mission statement of Valleys Kids is the same now as it was in these early days. *'Valleys Kids is a celebration of the achievements of individuals and communities who through trying different activities and having different experiences broaden their horizons and achieve their potential.'* This appears in much of the literature. It contains the gist of Valleys Kids answer to the call.

THE BIKE CLUB – THE INITIAL RESPONSE

The work of the Penygraig Projects and subsequently Valleys Kids is organic: it has evolved. It is deeply rooted, evolving from the needs of the community. With well-considered values, it arose from a collective passion focussed on a desire to improve the lives of young people and their families.

The first seeds of this initiative germinated in 1977. At that time, Howell Edwards, then a probation officer in the Rhondda, aided by money from a Job Creation scheme, was developing an innovative project, helping young clients into work as an alternative to a casework approach. Howell recalls that the Intermediate Treatment of young offenders at that time was quite enlightened: less punitive than today. The young people who were at risk of getting into serious trouble were seen as having needs and problems that required addressing. There was a concerted effort to encourage them to be involved in different pursuits. The first activity to be established was motorbike scrambling. This was seen as a challenging focus, which would appeal to a number of young people. While the riding of the bikes provided excitement and danger, it also provided an opportunity to learn about the mechanics. Howell saw this as a platform for forming relationships, a way of engaging with the boys: a method enabling them to work with adults and to form friendships with each other.

With the help of 2 volunteers, one a dad of a member of the group, they started a Bike Club, among other activities. This was a very popular activity for some time. Eventually, it proved difficult to keep going because of transportation problems and the difficulty of actually finding a place to scramble their bikes. Locally, one of the major factors that has lasted through the years is the name: The Bike Club. Officially, the venture was called the Penygraig Basement Project. Months later, when they moved to a new venue it became known as the Penygraig Community Project. However, for over 30 years the name that has lived on in the memory of the community is the Bike Club, encapsulating the fondness for the centre and the spirit of enthusiasm of that era.

Lesley, a friend of Audrey's, arrived at our meeting with an invitation card dated November 1979 and photographs of some of the members with the original bike. That experience lives on in her memory. The Prince's Trust donated money for that bike. Consequently, the invite was for some of the club members to meet H.R.H. Prince Charles, Prince of Wales. At first, six young people shared that much appreciated one motorbike.

Around the same time that Howell was developing this scheme, Margaret Jervis and Richard Morgan had moved south from Scotland with a plan to work with young people in the South Wales valleys. Margaret was a youth and community worker of long experience. A voluntary worker for many years, after attaining a specialist professional qualification in this field, she had managed youth and community projects in Aberdeenshire and Aberdeen city consecutively. Richard, a teacher, who grew up in Cynon Valley, had been involved in community art projects with young people in Liverpool before he moved to Aberdeen. Working together in St Katherine's, Aberdeen, they discovered that they had a shared vocation: common goals in creating ways to engage with and help young people in the community.

They arrived in South Wales in the period that was gradually leading up to the closure of the coalmines. They came with an idea of developing a community project, which would be run and managed by local people. However, they discovered very quickly that they were stepping back many years, professionally. At that time, the Youth Service in South Wales was predominantly based in schools and staffed by teachers. Richard was able to work in this field because he is a qualified teacher. He took up a temporary post in Maerdy at the head of the Rhondda Fach. Margaret, who was considered as highly skilled and experienced in youth work in Scotland, found the more conservative establishment in Wales considered her as unqualified because she did not come from a teaching background.

What this hurdle highlighted was the different and conflicting values in youth and community work in this period of time, the 1970s. Margaret and Richard's experience had shown them that the informal atmosphere of youth work did not always sit easily in the more formal and disciplined surroundings of a school. The approaches and skills of relating to young people in the different jobs come from a different perspective. Then, the ethos of the school driven youth work was to engage with youngsters during school hours and within the school term. Among Margaret and Richard's intentions was a plan to reach the young people that schools did not always reach; to make contact when they were more likely to be bored, or at a loose end. That meant being prepared to work unsocial hours, in evenings, at weekends, during the long summer holidays.

What transpired from that merging of ideals was a project which was exciting, unique, innovative and to the advantage of the greater community.

It was inevitable that Howell, Margaret and Richard should come across each other in this close community of the Rhondda. They had a common interest in young people, a shared belief that encouraged members of the community to take a responsibility for that neighbourhood. As well as this they had a combined desire to find a respectful and more flexible way of working with the young in the area; of reaching boys and girls where other agencies had not; of doing preventative youth work before the youngsters found themselves in serious trouble. In December 1977, Margaret, Richard and Howell met up, shared their visions of working with young people and discovered their views were compatible. What transpired from that merging of ideals was a project which was exciting, unique, innovative and to the advantage of the greater community.

Some of those interviewed from the first group of young people involved in this project remember a particular volunteer as great fun particularly on the trips away: Pauline Richards. At that time, Pauline was working as a secretary in the probation office. She had been a volunteer with Social Services for some time and became very involved with the Basement Club. Pauline was a volunteer from 1979 until 1983 when she took up full time employment with Penygraig Community Project, later going on to train as a youth and community worker in North Wales. Along with Howell, Margaret and Richard, she has been deeply involved, a key figure with the Valleys Kids projects from this time; now employed in a senior role within the organisation.

Today, Howell Edwards is Chairman of the Trustees; Margaret Jervis is Operational Director; Richard Morgan is Funding Director; and Pauline Richards, a Community Development Manager. It has taken a lot of passion, dedication, determination, challenging discussions and teamwork to progress from there and make Valleys Kids happen. With the assistance of many people, this initiative has grown, developed and lasted for over 33 years, helping thousands of people in the process.

DIGGING THE FOUNDATIONS

Margaret took up the post of youth worker in the Basement Project in January 1978. Richard joined her about 6 months later when his temporary post in Maerdy came to an end. For many years, until the project became more established, Margaret and Richard worked very hard sharing one salary between them.

The afore mentioned basement consisted of 2 small whitewashed rooms in the Penygraig Probation Office. The youngsters themselves, volunteers from the community, alongside Rhondda Social Services Department, the Day Training Centre and the Community Service Scheme, had converted the club premises from a coal cellar. The adults involved had an intention that although the project was started to help young people known to social services and the probation office, it should be expanded to include young people in the wider community of Penygraig. The response to the 'open door' youth club was immediate. It grew very quickly from 4 girls and 4 boys attending to over 40 people present in the basement on some evenings. There were now three main focuses of work in the Basement Project: open sessions, closed groups for the Intermediate Treatment clients and multi-agency groups.

After chatting to founders, members, volunteers and staff, the impression I was left with was that the open sessions of the Penygraig Basement Project were provided in a place where young people could attend, socialise, get involved in

The culture was embedded in the belief that the more responsibility you give young people, the more responsible they are likely to become.

some activities and be accepted for who they were. They were given certain boundaries like no drinking during project activities. At the same time they were also given a lot of freedom and encouraged to take responsibility for the running and development of that enterprise. As part of a community group, boys and girls were also consulted about future developments; they were part of the decision making process. The initial projects of what was to become Valleys Kids provided a venue where they were encouraged to try different things, to become more aware of their community: to expand their horizons. The culture was embedded in the belief that the more responsibility you give young people, the more responsible they are likely to become.

Being an innovative project, the colleagues involved seem prepared to take risks and go through quite a large learning curve. The annual report of 1978/79 refers to different challenges, particularly the method of running the project. The management of the club included everyone, fulltime staff, voluntary workers and young people. All were given the opportunity to have their voices heard. The adjective used to describe these meetings was '*arduous*' as many of the young people had not been seriously involved in taking part in such a decision making process, before. However, despite everyone talking at once during lengthy meetings, problems were aired, decisions were eventually taken, and plans made. The staff had worked hard and constructively at questioning people's expressed opinions. The initial response of the young in considering someone's misdemeanour was to be extremely retributive. The workers tried to create a tolerant atmosphere, accepting if not condoning certain behaviours. Mutual respect for each other was an expectation of the project.

'We were all treated as the same. We were encouraged to make decisions. The staff and the volunteers didn't appear to pull on their authority. I felt safe there. They treated us differently from schools. I learned in a different way. I learned more because we were having fun.'

Lesley recalls her experience of the Basement Project. She was about 15 years old when she joined and stayed involved for 2 or 3 years. *'It was a place where we could go and have a chat and enjoy ourselves in the right way – not hang about the streets. There was nothing else like it here in Penygraig. We were asked what we wanted to do. We were all treated as the same. We were encouraged to make decisions. The staff and the volunteers didn't appear to pull on their authority. I felt safe there. They treated us differently from schools. I learned in a different way. I learned more because we were having fun.'* Fun and having different experiences seem to have been key issues for these young people. She remembered many trips away from home, taking part in many activities, including horse riding, canoeing, rock climbing and photography; pursuits she had not tried before. As an adult looking back on that age *'in between a kid and an adult'*, Lesley commented that although she didn't realise it at the time, she believed that she had been taught different life skills by the approach of the project.

Central to the ethos of the Penygraig Projects was a belief in involving volunteers in the running of the community projects. In the early days, the service and commitment from many of these people was huge, and for some, that loyalty continues to this day to various degrees. Several reports over the years make it clear that without the support of volunteers there would have been no project. The organisation of Valleys Kids has benefited hugely from the dedication of these people who freely offered their services.

In return, many of those volunteering have expressed gratitude for this experience. A number reported that it helped raise their self-esteem. For some, this opportunity helped them go into further training and move back into work. Different people have returned to work for

'They enjoy a significant status because they are made to feel that what they do is important.'

the organisation as professionals at a later stage. At the present time approximately 30% of the staff employed at Valleys Kids have previously been volunteers. Over the years, Valleys Kids has offered opportunities for training and become a significant employer in an area where there continues to be few groundbreaking work solutions. Historically, the mining industry was the major focus of employment in the valleys. That central hub of occupation for the work force has not been replaced here, to this day.

Ross Davey and Anne Evans are 2 people who illustrate well the shifts that people have made between being volunteers and professionals. As a result of funding from the Manpower Services Commission to help people find work, both were employed by Penygraig Community project as youth workers in 1980/81. The scheme lasted for a year. Ross was one of the original youth club members of the Penygraig Basement Club before becoming a volunteer, helping with the move into Cross Street. After his period of employment at the project he moved back to the building trade for over 12 years. He has since returned to the Penygraig Project and has been employed as a youth and playworker at Valleys Kids for some time now. Anne, on the other hand returned to working as a nursery nurse but continued to come back as a volunteer for many years. She went to university in 2003, obtaining an Art degree and had to find evening work. Eventually, she joined the Penyrenglyn project for a few hours a week. She has worked full time for Valleys Kids since her graduation. Drawing from her own experience, Anne's comment sums up the attitude of the organisation to volunteers.

'They enjoy a significant status because they are made to feel that what they do is important.'

THE DRIVE OF THE 1980S

To understand the need for this organisation it is
necessary to take on board the impact of this decade on
the communities of the Rhondda. The coal pits closed
in 1985 after the defeat of the miners' strike of 1984-85.
Therefore, it was a time of great uncertainty and massive
unemployment. Many families had a hard time surviving
financially. In the second half of the decade, young men in
particular had great difficulty in finding work. According
to several of the people interviewed, the atmosphere in the
community was tense and very depressed. In the late 1980s
and the early 1990s, there was little expectation about
future employment.

In contrast, the last twenty years of 20th century were a time
of great enthusiasm and drive for the Penygraig Community
Project, as it was now known. Having been established in
the late 70s, it was in a good position to respond creatively
to the crisis, which gathered momentum and overwhelmed
the valleys' communities in the following decade. After
some initial funding came from the Manpower Services
Commission, it was followed with a grant from the Rainer
Foundation Intermediate Treatment Fund. Mid Glamorgan
County Council began grant aid in 1980 and continued to
support the project, over the years - as has its successor,
Rhondda Cynon Taff.

Records indicate that the work of the Basement Club had
fast outgrown the cramped space. The project accepted
an offer from Rhondda Borough Council to rent the old
Cooperative Society Offices at 1 Cross Street, Penygraig
at a peppercorn rate. The building had been empty for 10
years and was in a bad condition. It was agreed to renovate
and make this usable. Staff and volunteers tackled a lot
of this work. In the last 3 months of 1979 it was rewired,

walls were knocked down and a painting project was undertaken. The then young people who I interviewed described the hard work renovating the basement, (their part of the building) and the filthy state they got into doing it. Above all, they talked with pride about the sense of ownership, which lasts to this day for some. Everyone involved in the Penygraig Basement Project had been consulted about the move.

Around the same time, the project accepted a gift of the main hall of the Soar Ffrwdamos Chapel from the Welsh Baptist congregation led by Mrs Rhianydd Parry, a long time friend of Valleys Kids. Eventually the whole building became the property of Valleys Kids. This chapel was close to the other new premises. There were big problems with dry rot, so over a period of 6 years funds were raised for materials in order to tackle the upgrading of the building. The Community Industry and Community Programme did much of the renovation work. Again, there was a major commitment from volunteers. Ralph, one of the dads involved in working with the kids, fabricated and erected new steel work for the new upstairs floor in the chapel. Richard rewired the building for electricity. Running out of funds and urgently needing to repair the roof, Howell and his wife Eirlys found themselves dipping into savings planned for the arrival of their new baby.

Before we consider some more of the personal stories, perhaps the easiest way to portray the intense energy and commitment of this time is to quote straight from a Penygraig Community Project report called Working Together. Written in 1991, this is a reflection of the many achievements of this era.

1980

- Moved to the old Co-op. Offices, which had been converted, from a derelict building into an office, activity rooms, coffee bar and social area.
- Work with younger children began to expand and the junior youth club began.
- The parent and toddler group was established.

1981

We initiated a policy of integration of children with special needs.

- Jointly with the Education and Social services Departments the project established the Intermediate Treatment Centre at the Project. This innovative development was at the forefront of a strategy for work with adolescents at risk throughout the county.
- First Children's Show.

1982

- This proved to be an exciting year with a visit from Lord Hunt in February, and a visit from H.R.H. prince Charles in March.
- A successful Urban Aid application supported by Social Services meant a further member of staff joined the Project.

1984

- Using the local Labour Club as a venue we brought the first Community Theatre Company to the project.

1985

- With a grant from the Welsh Office the Miskin Project was established. This was set up to look at alternatives to care and custody for young people. At the end of the experimental period the Social Services Department assimilated this innovative work into the practice of the Adolescent Team.

1986

- A Women's Group was established and work has been carried on in cooperation with the Red Flannel video and film group and Advice work with a women's aid worker.
- This year also saw the development of the Middle Club for those young people who did not fit either Junior or Senior club.

1987

- Soar Ffrwdamos Centre was opened in November by H.R.H. Prince Charles. The former main hall of Capel Soar had been converted into a beautiful, multipurpose community centre, with a large upstairs hall, a large open plan social and multipurpose activity area along with smaller activity and store rooms. The congregation continued to use the vestry of the chapel for worship and the graveyard, which was an inaccessible jungle, was made into a garden. Work which had been limited by the facilities at Cross Street could now be developed. A programme of Theatre, Dance and Music events was established. The play activities we could offer to children were expanded.

The attitude of the
organisation was
always 'We can do it
if you help us.'

1988

- Return visit of Lord Hunt when he said, " Right from the beginning we spotted the need for this project.......... It is a model example and there is nothing quite like it in the Principality."

1989

- The purchase of the garages which lie between our two main buildings was completed. They are being converted into workshop and storage space.
- Inspection by H.M. Inspectors.

1990

- With the support of Rhondda Borough Council a grant from the Valleys Initiative Fund meant the transforming of the upstairs hall into a well equipped theatre.
- The latest development was the introduction of a series of films shown over the winter of 1990/91.

The Working Together Report claims that *'Each development has been in response to the community.'* As the project moved to Cross Street and the renovations continued, the demands from the community grew. The first summer playscheme had taken place in 1979. The success of that venture encouraged local people to ask for similar experiences of play all year round. Afterschool clubs developed in response to a community need. A Health Visitor who was working with a number of young Mums approached the Penygraig Community Project about starting a mothers and toddlers group. The attitude of the organisation was always *'We can do it if you help us.'*

Eirlys and Ruth, with young children of their own, ran the Mothers and Toddlers group. It was a novel idea in the area. The enthusiasm was huge but the money limited. Eirlys, now a retired teacher commented, *'We would never get away with it now, health and safety wise.'* Heat came from a one-bar electric fire. There was a 2-ring cooker. Old carpets were laid on the floor. People donated old tricycles. Rolls of wallpaper were cut up for children to paint on. Those involved seemed not to care about the 'make-do for now' atmosphere. The group proved very popular, putting pressure on the organisation for more provision. This opportunity offered stimulating play, a chance for the youngsters to socialise and time for parents to chat to others in similar circumstances.

In the meantime, while all this was going on, Pauline moved from being a volunteer, joining the staff in 1983. Amongst doing many other things, she followed an already established tradition and wrote and produced 3 children's shows. These usually had a cast of about 100 kids and 4 adults. They were community events, with volunteers making costumes, arranging music, and creating scenic designs. Adults of today who were children then still recount many tales of these times. This was the origin of the ArtWorks department becoming established as part of the Valleys Kids' picture.

As can be seen from the above extract, the initiative of the organisation attracted the interest of some high profile visitors during these years. There were visits from both Lord Hunt and H.R.H. Prince Charles. Lord Hunt came twice during that period and Prince Charles has had continued contact with Valleys Kids, as well as Prince William. In turn, their interest opened ears and has helped keep the image of the organisation high in people's awareness. These relationships have encouraged doors to open elsewhere, helping Valleys Kids develop and expand to help other communities.

A report from H. M. Inspectors on the Penygraig Community Project, Rhondda, Mid Glamorgan (Autumn Term 1989) concludes:

'The Penygraig Community Project has good reason to be proud of its achievements and the progress it is continuing to make in responding to the communal needs of the district it serves. The development of the project and its clientele is enhanced in particular by the quality of its premises, the effective deployment of resources, the collaboration achieved among the core team and volunteers, and the pervasive vitality, commitment and warmth of those involved.'

A JOINT APPROACH

As indicated in the report about the developments of the 1980s, the multi agency work that was started in the original Penygraig Basement Project continued in its new home at Cross Street. While the wider youth and community work was evolving, the Intermediate Treatment Centre for adolescents in especially difficult circumstances extended its work in the ground floor of the same building. Teachers, probation workers, social workers and youth and community workers cooperated, finding a compatible method of working together in the same building; helping young people from all backgrounds improve their lives.

Phil Evans, now Director of Social Services for the Vale of Glamorgan and a Trustee of Valleys Kids, was employed by the Penygraig Community Project and its partners between 1981 and 1992 to create this groundbreaking project working with children at risk. (It was jointly funded by both Social Services and Education). The project was grant funded and therefore time limited. However, the original period of 3 years was extended to 5 and later 7 years.

From the start, the centre was set up as an integral part of Penygraig Community Project, allowing some of the most disadvantaged children and young people from both the Rhondda Valleys to experience the special environment, which had been created in this project. Phil explained that at this time children who had committed offences were often sent away from the valleys to residential care; a good proportion had experienced imprisonment. In those days it was much easier for young offenders to find themselves in care or detention centres. Some were sent away for 'offences' that amounted to little more than non-attendance at school. Others were involved in heavy criminal behaviour and seen as being beyond control. Many were there as a result of family breakdown, learning disabilities, mental health problems and above all, as a result of living in poverty. The task of this intermediate treatment centre was to repatriate these young people back into their communities and prevent others from following the same path. The Penygraig Project was an ideal situation for the Centre's day-care programme and evening groups as it was designed to provide for all young people. The kids in the Intermediate Treatment Centre were accepted as part of that community with little trouble.

Their scheme was able to stay separate with its own social and educational programme during the day and yet encourage the young people to merge with the other activities in other parts of the project in the evenings and weekends. The day care programme took place on 4 days of the week with formal teaching, social education, arts and crafts activities, group work and psychodrama. A small

For young people who often had had little structure in their lives or sometimes too much, this initiative gave them the opportunity to be part of a community that made them feel welcome.

team of adults worked directly with the turnover group of about 8 young people at a time in day care and many evening groups and holiday scheme. Phil (whose work title was Warden), a teacher, a social worker, a cook/ cleaner and a secretary all brought their own considerable and diverse skills in relating to young people in trouble. There were also closed evening groups specifically for 10 to 15 of the intermediate treatment youngsters in which Pauline and other volunteers were involved. As part of the integration scheme with the wider project, they learned about photography with Richard and took part in other youth club activities with Ross.

For young people who often had had little structure in their lives or sometimes too much, this initiative gave them the opportunity to be part of a community that made them feel welcome. It was a real achievement for them to just turn up in the same place day after day. They did far more, taking much of the responsibility for making the centre a place of refuge and a place where they could learn for themselves. Previously, many had been excluded from schools or passed around the different services in the area. As well as learning to relate to adults and their peers, they discovered they could play a crucial role in helping each other to manage problematic areas in their lives. The advantage of being in the informal setting of the Penygraig Project was that everybody experienced positive and informal relationships, not the use of heavy authority. The support between the adults and young and among the peers was encouraged to be reciprocal.

In keeping with the overall values of the Penygraig Project, it gave the kids the opportunity to discover and work on their talents. Some found they were good at helping and supporting the others in the group. A young person from a family of four generations of criminals found a flair for writing stories after Richard helped the Centre pioneer the use of computers in the classroom. A few girls found much enjoyment working on and riding motorbikes; one or two boys discovered an interest in making stuffed toys. The kids would spend one day a week in other parts of the community. Residential trips to outdoor pursuit centres throughout Wales and to London were a special treat. Through the Intermediate Treatment Centre, Penygraig Community Project was able to purchase some garages that were located between the 2 converted buildings. Initially, they were used for the Motor Project, which was a scheme to help young people involved with car crime to understand and appreciate cars.

As part of the learning process in being part of a community, they were encouraged to take part in the decision-making and management of the wider organisation. For some, the period of criminal activity was a phase. Others needed a much longer period of support from the team. Sometimes, it took a couple of years before they could go back to school, train at a technical college or find employment in communities where opportunities were hard to find.

Of course, not all the young people found their way to productive and fulfilled lives. For some of them other influences and adversities remained too powerful. However, the Centre made a major contribution in helping to influence the reduction of the use of custody and punitive forms of residential care for children and young people in the Rhondda. It also provided a place where many troubled kids found they belonged.

WIDENING THE RETURN

In Chapter 6 we will be catching up with Penygraig in the 21st century. However, before we venture further, let us look at the Penygraig of this time. Julie Parsons, who was also a volunteer for many years, trained as a playworker with Penygraig Community Project and was also a resident of the village. She and her friend Jenny, remember several more shops in the main street than now. The Cooperative Society was prominent in Penygraig with several stores in the area. At one point, there were also 2 banks that no longer exist. Julie believes that you got to know your neighbours more at that time. Now, new people have moved into the area and more people go out to work. The community does not seem as close as it use to be. Cars were less in number so children were able to play relatively safely on the streets.

The action plan (1993/1994) of the Penygraig Community Project describes the township in this way:

'... It has a population of 7000 of which approximately 18% are aged between 14 and 25 years and 20% are over retirement age. The appearance is of a typical South Wales mining town established in the 19th century. It is estimated that 10% of the housing stock lacks one or more basic amenities. Unemployment stands at 12% overall but higher levels are recorded among young men in their early 20s. Family incomes are lower than the Mid Glamorgan average and the area call on health and welfare services is high. In a recent Welsh Office report on deprivation, the area featured as 9th worst in Wales.'

Meanwhile, the intensity and pace of work in the Penygraig Community Project did not abate in the new decade of the 1990s. Miranda Ballin, now coordinator of the Artswork team came from Spectacle Theatre to develop a drama project working with the young people of the valleys, Margaret and Pauline continued the more informal youth and community work of the project and Richard developed CAT (Community Access to Technology). This was an early programme introducing computer skills aimed particularly at helping people find work.

Also, while continuing to develop its work in Penygraig, the project started to look further afield and widen its perimeters. Members of staff began to reach out to other communities in the County that was to become known as Rhondda Cynon Taf. The metamorphosis of the Penygraig Community Project into Valleys Kids was gradually evolving introduced by the development of playwork. In fact, John Lenaghan goes as far to state that *'the play project was the midwife of Valleys Kids, taking the ethos of the organisation beyond Penygraig.'* (At that time, John was a Community Development worker with Rhondda Social Services.) Along with others, he was involved in discussions about the need to expand the access to playschemes in Rhondda. These discussions eventually led to the setting up of a steering committee to Rhondda Play Project.

Marianne was another innovative key worker to take up employment with Penygraig Community Project. She arrived in 1992 to develop playwork for the organisation. A grant from Children in Need helped secure her role in managing and supporting a team of outreach playworkers. She jokes that she got the job because she helped wash the dishes while waiting for interview. Actually, she was more than well qualified for the job. In expressing this, she was highlighting the organisation's expectation that employees do not hide behind the boundaries of their professional position. The road to community regeneration requires a hands-on approach for all. She stated that the management give members of staff a lot of scope to be inventive and creative. In return, they are expected to be part of the wider team and not precious about their particular focus of work. The expectation is that when the situation demands it, colleagues roll up their sleeves and get on with it, supporting each other.

As Marianne supported Rhondda Play Forum and developed play provision in the valleys she discovered that her skills and ways of working provided a good tool to engage with the community. Initially, Penygraig Community Project hired a playbus from the National Play Association so that she and Debra (administrator/playworker) could identify and visit communities that were struggling to provide good play. In this process they got to know families and neighbourhoods and linked into other professional teams. Among those contacts effective relationships were created with health work teams. They worked together, starting initiatives to help improve the health of young mums and babies.

In April 1996 Bridges was created as an outreach project. Its aim was to continue the work of Penygraig Community Project in identified areas of Rhondda Cynon Taf. The team responsible for developing this project consisted of Pauline as Community Development Worker, Marianne as Play Development Worker and Debra as Playworker along with some sessional playworkers. With a remit to make contact with 10 other areas and carry out a needs assessment, it used a newly owned community bus to do the original research work as well as provide play, youth work and support for adults for deprived areas. Among the many outcomes of this project were the developments of the Penyrenglyn and Rhydyfelin Community Projects described in following chapters.

CARRYING IT FORWARD

It is obvious from the evidence of the people with whom I met that the original organisation had its ear close to ground and heard very clearly what many of the needs of the community were. That call was extensive and it came with a sense of urgency. As the work was introduced into other areas and as the charity expanded, the project could no longer call itself just the Penygraig Community Project. An advisor was brought in to recommend ways of managing change. After a long and complicated multi-community consultation, the title Valleys Kids was chosen to embrace all of the work they undertook to help children and their families in South Wales. This covered all of the community bases and the work of the specialists who travelled between them, as well as in other areas. As the following pages will illustrate the organisation grew from a small 'family' establishment with a common aim, to an employer of over 50 people at its busiest times.

Several changes occurred towards the end of the 1990s. The approach of Children's Services to working with young people altered and funding for the work with children with special needs ran out. So, the Intermediate Team left the Penygraig Community Project. At the cusp of the new millennium, the Community Projects of Penyrenglyn, Rhydyfelin and Pen Dinas came on board, the Artwork team gradually expanded, family work was developed further, and a community advocate was employed. Plans were also underway for the transformation of the Penygraig Community Centre into a state of the art community building.

Inevitably, with such a rapid swelling out of some of its work there were some growing and adjustment pains. Because of enlargement and the consequential need to

The longevity of many of the staff, the devotion of many volunteers, the loyalty of the neighbourhoods and the continuing quality of work illustrate that this is a solid organisation committed to regenerating communities particularly for the benefit of the young and their families.

manage change, Valleys Kids has become more hierarchical than the Penygraig Community Projects were. However, in keeping that structure relatively flat, it has been able to stay fairly flexible despite its size. The longevity of many of the staff, the devotion of many volunteers, the loyalty of the neighbourhoods and the continuing quality of work illustrate that this is a solid organisation committed to regenerating communities particularly for the benefit of the young and their families. As funding for some pioneering projects runs out or as communities' needs change, it is able to adjust its direction and create more innovative schemes to the advantage of different neighbourhoods.

The old mining communities in which Valleys Kids work have some resemblances but all are unique with different needs. Community regeneration requires a local response. As will be described in following chapters, the different projects have a similar heart but have developed their own character. Several of the people interviewed believe that what keeps Valleys Kids anchored is an adherence to the core principles that were established from the beginning. These have been carried forward, containing the projects as the organisation has adapted to growth.

According to the original pioneers, those values include the following:

- **A vision that people of all ages respond creatively to opportunity and new experiences.**
- **A belief that all can contribute to the greater good (young and old from all backgrounds).**
- **An aim to help individuals feel that their voice is important; that their input is essential and they have the right to take the organisation to task if decisions are seen as wrong.**

- **A purpose to help people feel good about themselves and to believe that they are important.**
- **A knowledge that given the right support, everyone has the capacity to achieve his or her potential.**
- **A conviction that collective solutions to individual, family and neighbourhood problems are better.**
- **An encouragement of the concept of mutuality – that we are all in this together: an attitude that, 'We will help you if you help us.'**
- **A respect for the values of the local neighbourhood.**
- **A trust that the more responsibility you give young people, the more responsible they are likely to become.**
- **An expectation that people and property are treated with respect.**
- **A commitment that no matter who people are, they deserve the best of what the organisation can give them. No child or adult should be deprived of opportunities on financial grounds**.

In essence what this organisation provides is a network of friendship – well thought out 'professional' friendship where the ethos and the governance of the establishment are respected and the training and skills of the staff are honoured. Yet, the relationships with members of the community are encouraged to be on a par. Richard Wilkinson and Kate Pickett, in their book about the need for social equality (entitled The Spirit Level), describe this kind of friendship: *'It is about reciprocity, mutuality, sharing, social obligations, co-operation and recognition of each others needs.'*

Growing from the bedrock and success of the Penygraig Community projects, this venture became known as Valleys Kids on the 24th March 1999. The story of its creative response to the needs of young people, families and communities continues as follows.

PART TWO

Echoes in the Valleys

CHAPTER 3

Hearing from the Penyrenglyn Community Project

'Just because you come from somewhere doesn't mean you have to behave in a certain way.'

This statement came from Jonathan who is now employed as a youth and playworker by Valleys Kids at the Penyrenglyn Community Project. He grew up in the housing estate Mount Libanus, in Penyrenglyn, part of the Treherbert ward at the head of the Rhondda Fawr. Mount Libanus was the first focus of the Bridges project mentioned in the last chapter. In the 1980s and 90s it had gained a reputation for problem families, drugs and violence. Locally it became known as the Ranch. People who lived there were stigmatised for doing so and became known as the Ranchers, or sometimes even - the smelly Ranchers. According to Jonathan: *'The people living in the terraced housing nearby didn't want to know us.'* Police failed to turn up on several occasions when called to sort out a disturbance.

However, although he describes the area as rough, with drugs everywhere and regular fights taking place, Jonathan remembers it as a safe place to grow up. Different families supported each other through the hard times. Individual families looked after their own. *' Nobody messed with me because my family was big.'*

'This is where I grew up and where I belong. I care about what happens to the estate. I want to give kids the same opportunity that I was given.'

Jonathan's story is a good one to help illustrate the influence of Valleys Kids' role on helping change the path of life for so many; in this case, through the Penyrenglyn Community Project. He is now 26 years old. He joined the Middle Youth Club there when he was 14. Living across the road, he remembers playing hell and having to be put out of the club most nights. However, his life started to turn around when he was 15 and he became a volunteer helping run the playscheme for younger kids. It seems his involvement with the Penyrenglyn centre gave him the nudge to turn in the right direction. At 16 he was picked as one of four from Valleys Kids to go to Camp America in Maine. This was a summer camp usually attended by wealthy young people. Valleys Kids raised the money to cover the costs. While he was in the United States, Jonathon experienced for the first time such activities as whale-watching, camping and white-water rafting. He made friends from different backgrounds, many of whom he is still in touch with today via facebook.

It was an experience full of fun - and it was much more than that. It raised his expectations. It helped him believe he was worth more in life. It opened doors. Continuing to volunteer with the Penyrenglyn Project, he went to college for 2 years and received his NNEB to be a nursery nurse. Through the United Nations Association, he went to Rome and helped renovate a really run down youth club. He has obtained his NVQ in youthwork and is aiming for a degree. For a while he was a part time employee of Valleys Kids: now he works for them fulltime. He states: *'This is where I grew up and where I belong. I care about what happens to the estate. I want to give kids the same opportunity that I was given.'* It is important to acknowledge that for different reasons, many of the adults close to Jonathan had not worked during his lifetime. He has altered the pattern. The change he has made has had a ripple effect and his family enjoys more stability in the present time.

Jonathan is really appreciative of what he has been given and has achieved through his own hard work. He considered some of his childhood friends who were not given the same opportunities. He feels he has grown up while they haven't. Some are in prison, some in trouble with drugs. At best, some have chosen to have babies very early in life and others have settled for a job they do not enjoy. They were unaware or did not believe that they had choices. Jonathon says that they didn't have plans, didn't know they could have higher aspirations; they have not had the same encouragement to envisage wider horizons.

Jonathan has had that opportunity and has used it to break with the assumed stereotype of the community in which he grew up. It has taken personal courage accompanied by the support of others to develop that possibility of change into skills that will benefit the future of others, as well as his own.

THE DROWNING OF A COMMUNITY VOICE

Treherbert is the most northerly township in the Rhondda Fawr and recorded in the 2001 census as having a population of 6011. The people who live in there tend to be self-deprecating. Perhaps as we start to understand some of their history we can conclude that events of the 20th century have contributed to that inward-looking criticism.

Like all the other communities in the Rhondda valleys, Treherbert is a former mining village that was at its economic peak between 1850 and 1920. Not only did local people have to cope with the closure of nearby pits which gradually started to wind down from around the 1950s, they had some of their freedom of movement restricted in the 1960s when Beeching closed many railways. In the case of Treherbert, the tunnel under the mountain through which the railway travelled, was closed to neighbouring towns and valleys. This much used method of transport had taken passengers and goods through to the Vale of Neath and Port Talbot. The termination of the railway line prevented families who had married on the other side of the mountain from having easy access to each other. The mountain road was frequently being closed because of landslides or bad weather. Up until that point, because travelling was accessible, some of the population who lived in this area chose Neath or Port Talbot as their local market town. They were drawn more to the neighbouring valley. Whereas, people who lived further south in the Rhondda valleys tended to veer towards Pontypridd for their shopping.

The shutting down of the tunnel demanded that the people from Treherbert and surrounding district change their focus. When that part of the railway was in action they had an easier route into the outside world than some of the other communities in the Rhondda. The closure caused the residents to see themselves much more as a restricted heads-of-the-valley population than previously. To quote one of the present day residents, *'We live at the dead-end of the valley'*.

On recollecting these memories, some of the present-day older people attending the Penyrenglyn centre felt quite strongly that their needs had been disregarded, at the time. Their affiliation with towns outside the valley was quite strong and the closure restricted their travels. The suspicion of indifference to their way of life was reinforced by another scheme of the time to flood the upper valley for use as a reservoir. This plan did not materialise but it reinforced a conclusion that the people and communities of the upper Rhondda mattered little to the people in power; that their voices were drowning under the insensitivity of decision makers.

Therefore, when considering the plight of the Mount Libanus estate it is important to see it as a neighbourhood spurned by a larger community that also was suffering from a feeling of being discounted or under-valued. It was a community placed outside the larger community: socially as well as geographically.

Originally, the Mount Libanus estate was built in the still fairly affluent times of the 1950s for the workers employed in the factories in the industrial area of neighbouring Treorchy. As these factories closed down or were relocated to other areas, employees moved or became unemployed. Many of the dwellings were left empty. The vacant houses of the Mount Libanus estate became one of the local council's answers to solving the wider housing problems in the 1970s. They shipped in families from all over the area with poor support, poor finances, poor job prospects and many social problems. The plan backfired for a while because the council had failed to recognise the need for an infrastructure of support when building a new community. Pockets of problem families clustered together on the estate and ruled the roost. They became very powerful and intimidated others. This was when the neighbourhood received a reputation for violence and drugs.

As industry moved out of the valleys in the wake of the closure of the mines, transport deteriorated and became more expensive making it more difficult for people to move around the area. The estate bus became irregular, running every 2 hours during the day and not at all in the evenings. While it was possible to catch buses on the main routes this was difficult for young mums in particular when pushing prams up the very steep hill. Census figures of that era

showed that 61% of households in the area had no car. Those who lived there became quite confined.

Built on the side of a mountain in the community of Penyrenglyn, Mount Libanus estate is adjoined by an area of older terraced housing. According to a report from the Penyrenglyn Project in October 1995, the estate was made up of some 229 dwellings consisting of 2 and 3 bedroomed accommodations. Tenants in receipt of state benefit occupied 206 of those semidetached properties. Employment was inaccessible to the majority. Many families were suffering from chronic ill health.

Over time, empty houses became derelict, covered with graffiti, full of rubbish including used needles that had been used for injecting heroin. At one time, the Mount Libanus estate had become so run down that the council's plan was to demolish most of the housing scheme. The morale of the people living there was perceived as low but as will be discussed later in the chapter, many wanted to keep on living there. It was their home and they wanted a say in the matter. Gradually with the support of the project, they found unity and the courage to be assertive about their needs.

THE RAISING OF HEADS

The Bridges Project mentioned in the previous chapter started to make in-roads into this community leading to the formation of the Penyrenglyn Project. The initial invitation for help occurred in 1992 in response to health visitors expressing concern that they were spending a disproportionate amount of time on the estate. A study revealed marked health deficits particularly with mothers and young children. The report drawn from some

'The vision of this group was that the Penyrenglyn Project would improve the quality of life of young children, and adults of Penyrenglyn and area.'

research done by the health visitors drew a conclusion: *' The research revealed that the study group of mothers were 4 years younger at time of first pregnancy, had fewer supportive partners, had more children within the family and were more likely to live in cramped housing. Unemployment levels were over twice as high in the study group, pregnancies were less likely to be planned, primary immunisations were likely to be delayed or missed, less children were breast fed and more babies were given solids before being 3 months of age.'*

This community initiative continued to grow out of a concern that arose through a number of statutory agencies, voluntary organisations and individuals who were involved in the Mount Libanus housing estate. Through inter-agency discussions a working group with representatives from Social Services, Health, Education, Housing, the Tenants and Residents Association and the Penygraig Community Project was established. According to a development plan of the time called Forward Together: *'The vision of this group was that the Penyrenglyn Project would improve the quality of life of young children, and adults of Penyrenglyn and area.'* This would be achieved through the participation of local people in the development of the community activities and the improvement of the environment in which they lived. The continuing mantra for organisations that came under the umbrella of what was to become Valleys Kids was: *'We will help you if you help us.'* There was an expectation of a mutuality of support.

A number of activities were developed in the early days, beginning in September 1992. In the ensuing years the project was placed in many venues including the local infant school, the social services family home, the Treherbert Youth centre and the Bridges Project mobile play bus. A drop-in baby clinic, holiday playschemes, women's groups, a community drop-in morning, computer classes, a mobile needle exchange were all arranged by health, social services, TEDS (the local Drug and Alcohol advisory service), the tenants and residents association and the Penygraig Community project. Crucial to the project, volunteers were identified and involved in different sessions.

Julie Spiller was appointed as Project Coordinator and after much hard work, negotiation and successful fundraising by the forerunner of Valleys Kids (the Penygraig Community Project), the Penyrenglyn Community Centre was opened. Rhondda Borough housing department leased the project 4 estate houses, 2 of which were converted into that community centre. It had become increasingly apparent that the project needed a visible and continued presence on the estate where a variety of professional and more informal resources could be easily accessed: a base where the community could come together.

As the doors opened, the response from the community was immediate. A group of disaffected young people became involved early on in the project. They volunteered to help with the renovation work of the centre and did much of the painting of the building. They formed the nucleus of the Youth Club. Groups of volunteers became involved and established, organising and running different activities. The health visitors were pleased with the regular attendance of the baby clinic.

Local residents were being heard and valued. They were involved and contributing to their own betterment, as well as that of their neighbourhood. For the first time in many years several were able to lift their heads and look life in the eye.

'We believe it is essential to involve local people in the planning, management and staffing of community provision.'

Dave Adamson then director of the Regional Research programme commented in a survey done on the estate by Glamorgan University. *'It is clear, both from the interviews with professionals practising in the locality and from focus group discussions with residents that the Penyrenglyn Project has made significant change in the quality of life for residents. As well as the physical availability of resources there are key changes in people's confidence and a development of more positive attitudes and high self-esteem.'*

KNOWING HOW TO LISTEN

The Penygraig Community Project, which initially steered this project, had a clearly stated vision of involving and consulting members of the community in their future. *'We believe it is essential to involve local people in the planning, management and staffing of community provision. This will happen from the outset.'*

One of the greatest challenges in trying to engage with a community that has become alienated is in learning how to best communicate with the people involved. Julie, coordinator of the project since the building first opened, believes the difficulty in connecting with the community had partly arisen because the people living on the estate were afraid and suspicious of professionals. They felt *'twp'* or stupid around the people who came to help. Trust was an issue and had to be earned by those serving the community. Marianne, one of the founders of the Bridges Project believed they had to learn to ask questions differently. She saw it as essential that the community support workers were not seen to parachute in knowing all the answers. At the same time, having babies herself, she saw it as important to challenge some of the families' preconceived ideas of raising children. Both she and Julie saw their role as community development workers as placed somewhere between the other professionals involved and the local people: sometimes acting as intermediaries. Most often, they supported residents when they found the courage to speak their mind about different issues.

They discovered very quickly that those living on the estate were more likely to open up over a cup of tea in the atmosphere of the community centre than in a surgery or in their own home where they could feel judged by professional advisors. The ambiance of the converted building is welcoming and warm. Local people found it easier to discuss their concerns about their children or different health issues in the more relaxed, more informal surroundings of the new venue.

Julie became aware that the men on the estate were uncomfortable with their partners being so involved with the centre. Changing attitudes were altering the way relationships worked. She deliberately walked up and down the streets talking to people in their gardens, engaging the men in conversation and winning their trust, encouraging them to become involved, too. The centre now has groups for men and activities in which they take part. Some of the male population also participate as volunteers.

Ceri, who is caretaker, environmental worker, youth worker and jack of all trades at the centre saw the role of the project as an advocate for the people on the estate: standing up for their right to be heard. So often in the early days the general complaint from the residents was, *'Nobody listens to us anyway.'* For those people who had been intimidated by the louder cliques on the estate, support from the centre gave those who were silenced a

It gave them a voice, a sense of having an involvement in their own futures.

chance to step up and not feel outnumbered. It gave them a voice, a sense of having an involvement in their own futures. Ceri believes that this helped raise confidence and that all things in life become easier with confidence.

As soon as the centre opened, inhabitants of the estate were at the door asking for help with different problems. In the first week Julie was asked for help on many topics from finding out how to get a knob for a cooker to serious health issues and debt problems. The centre has become the first port of call for many on the estate for a variety of problems. If the staff at the project can help solve the difficulty they will; if it needs specialist attention they will support while referring on to a relevant agency.

FINDING A COLLECTIVE VOICE

'Working in partnership' is a much-coined phrase of recent years in the world of community regeneration. In fact, the survival of the Mount Libanus estate is due to the joined-up support shared between agencies like Children's Services, Health, TEDs, the University of Glamorgan, and Community Education alongside the Local Tenants and Residents Association supported by the Penyrenglyn Community Project. It is an early example of how crucial this method of working is in the communities of the Rhondda valleys in helping them heal.

In the mid 1990s, shortly after the opening of the Penyrenglyn Project it was revealed that the local council was considering demolishing the majority of houses on the estate and relocating the residents. Passions were aroused and regular meetings took place involving some of the organisations mentioned above. Local people became central in taking the initiative to fight for the survival of

'You can want a better life, you have the right to expect a better life; indeed, you can reach for a better life.'

their community. Collectively with the support of the project, they found their voice to state their needs.

Initially, what had not been recognised was that there was a large nucleus of residents who had lived in that area for 20 to 30 years. There was a stable population whose right to be heard had been silenced by the events mentioned above but they were now quite clear that didn't want to move. They were able to articulate their requirements, that they stay and that they wanted improvements made to the area in which they lived. They fought for this and they won. About 118 houses were pulled down. Those that remain are greatly enhanced. Today, some homes belong to Rhondda Housing (a housing association); some come under Rhondda Cynon Taf Borough Council; both these agencies rent out their properties to local residents. Other houses on the estate are privately owned. Interestingly, vandalism has practically been eradicated in this area. The physical changes have greatly boosted the morale of the Mount Libanus estate.

Julie sees the modernising of the buildings as symbolic as well as necessary. In helping the residents achieve their goal of improving their home environment, it sent a message. *'You can want a better life, you have the right to expect a better life; indeed, you can reach for a better life.'*

IMPROVING LIFE FOR THE YOUNG

As Jonathan's story represents, the changing mind-set of the community helped start raise aspirations for the children of the locality. For them, life did not have to stay the same as before. The pattern of oppression and defeat formed in earlier generations could be discontinued, uplifted and redesigned. New ways of living could be found.

Most children become involved at the project from a very early age, usually when they join the mother and baby club. From there they can progress to preschool playgroup, to afterschool club, to homework club, to middle youth club and then to senior youth club.

Caroline, who has been a youth worker at the Penyrenglyn Project for a decade enjoys her work in the close-knit community. She sees the children who attend in the present day as different from the ones who were first involved 10 years ago. In her opinion, the original youngsters were harder then, rougher, tougher – real street kids. In the last few years several families have been able to enjoy an improved lifestyle. More recently, some young people have 2 parents who are working so they have more financially and materially. Life is much easier that way; or it has been for a while. Once more, employment is becoming more difficult. The financial atmosphere is changing back as the latest recession kicks in. More people have been visiting the centre, seeking help in dealing with debt problems, again.

Most children become involved at the project from a very early age, usually when they join the mother and baby club. From there they can progress to preschool playgroup, to afterschool club, to homework club, to middle youth club and then to senior youth club. They can stay involved from being a baby until well into their teens or early 20s – and then there are different activities for adults. The centre is open on 7 days a week. While being involved with the different clubs, many choose to drop-in for a chat. Sometimes this can be just a casual conversation. On occasion, they might want to discuss some really serious stuff.

I met with 2 small groups of young people who are involved with the Penyrenglyn Project. Katy, Sicourry and Shanon from the Middle Youth Club; Dani (13), Dean(14), Lee (20) and Kim (19) from Senior Youth.

When discussing the importance of the project with them, what came high on that list was the appreciation of having a safe place to go, to meet friends and have fun. Just as valuable was having a venue and people who they could trust to discuss issues that were of a sensitive nature. Both groups appeared unanimous in believing there were no other venues where they were treated with such respect. As well as being able to talk to the youth workers, they appreciated the input of Jane, nurse and Valleys Kids' specialist in sexual health. One of the most important messages heard by the younger girls in the group was, *'If a boy don't treat you tidy, you are best staying away.'*

Dean volunteered that the project had helped him learn to talk one - to – one and encouraged him be less shy. He had been referred to the project about 3 years ago when he was involved in fighting and *'other anti-social stuff'*. He was proud to say that since he got involved with the project he has not been in trouble once.

Dani commented that her parents had benefited from the project because they got a break from her! She understood that Julie had helped her Mam and Dad *'become more strict'* with her. She appeared to appreciate the tighter boundaries. The meetings helped her get on with her parents much better than before.

As the centre has taken root in the community, the young people have learned that as well as being given long-term support they are expected to take some ownership for their community, to give back to it. Opposite the community centre is an area of pine forest owned by the Forestry Commission. Working with this organisation, under Ceri's guidance the local young people have learned to enjoy and learn from the environment, while taking care of it. They were asked for a wish list of how they would like to see their forest develop. It was emphasised that most of what they requested would be achieved gradually over time, if possible. To this date, they have built a barbeque, fire-pit, and pathways through the trees. Naval cadets helped clear the woods while teaching survival skills.

The young people love the outdoor experience and have become very protective over it. Setting fire to the mountains is a big problem in the South Wales valleys perhaps because fire is treated as a taboo subject with the young; something they had to be protected from. In the forestry project, under supervision the children are taught to treat fire with respect. They are allowed to explore it by toasting marshmallows in the flames, for example. According to the Penyrenglyn project, the fire brigade is pleased to report that they have not been called up to that area for many years now. Meanwhile, young people are still setting fire to moorland in other parts of the valleys.

Not only have the youngsters learned to respect fire, they have a better regard for the environment around them than previous generations. This has grown through their efforts in keeping the community tidier. This has had a positive influence on adults, too. Fly tipping has greatly reduced. One of the elderly was heard to comment on her newly found admiration for the young. Although they are loud and hang around in big groups, their care for the environment has helped her see that they are assets to the community.

THE PENYRENGLYN PROJECT TODAY

Early in the present millennium, a group of young people from the estate, along with youth worker Christian Perry, made a video called Not Ready for Drowning. It described the shift of change in this Rhondda valley community as *'moving from despair to hope and from diabolical to desirable'*. One of the recorded voices in this film foresaw the transition as making the residents less invisible. Indeed, a process of being more noticeable had started and has continued over the years.

As the neighbourhood housing was upgraded, Valleys Kids raised the money to modernise the community centre. H.R.H. the Prince of Wales opened the conversion in 2003. It is busy, used well by the local community. The activities there have attracted many from the wider community so the centre has become a vehicle for integrating the people of the estate with the extended population in Treherbert. Not only are the people of Mount Libanus estate acknowledged by the people in the terraced houses, they are more accepted by the wider population of the upper valley. Both adults and children can be seen sharing activities together.

Mount Libanus estate has changed beyond recognition since the 1990s. Valleys Kids' small team of staff and volunteers have played a large part in influencing and supporting this change. Physically, under Rhondda Housing, RCT and private owners, with the input of the local tenants association, the area has become much more attractive. The empty derelict houses have gone. The appearance of the remaining houses has been raised to a higher standard and gardens look well kept. The atmosphere has been lifted; there is a pride of occupancy. The outlook on to the forests and mountains is stunning.

Perhaps now the residents can lift their heads and actually see the beauty of their surroundings. In the past, when weighed down by their individual and community depression, it was difficult for them to appreciate that, fully.

A lot of progress has been made in the regeneration of this community. There is still more that can happen. Asking Julie what she considers as the greatest achievements of the Penyrenglyn Community Project, the reply was as follows. *'When people say 'no' to me; when they don't go along blindly with what I suggest; when they have the courage to have their own opinions.'*

CHAPTER 4

Listening to the Rhydyfelin Community Project

'School was where we went to be taught. The youth club was where we could talk. We could discuss anything there.'

This quotation came from 2 young professional women in their early 20s; both original members of the senior youth club in the Ilan centre in Rhydyfelin. Ther names are Kayleigh and Kylie.

These words bring into focus the different kind of relationship that young people have with the staff of Valleys Kids compared with those working in the statutory organisations. The quotation highlights a different level of engagement with individuals and illustrates the need for an organisation such as Valleys Kids, which is rooted deep in the heart of the community. We will study some of the effects of this specialist approach throughout this chapter.

First, it is important to have some understanding of the history and topography of the area in which these young people grew up.

A HILLSIDE COMMUNITY

Found in the county borough of Rhondda Cynon Taf, Rhydyfelin Community Project is the furthest south of Valleys Kids' neighbourhood initiatives. It is the only one of the Valleys Kids' centres that is not placed within the Rhondda Valleys. Instead, it lies within the district of Taf Ely and in the Pontypridd ward of Rhydyfelin and Ilan. Pontypridd, the principal town of RCT, lies 2 miles to its northwest. Being only 10 miles from the capital, it is nearest to Cardiff with easy access to the city by road and rail.

Rhydyfelin is sited along the eastern banks of the River Taf. In the 19th century, it grew from a hamlet due to its geographic location along the Glamorganshire Canal, which conveyed iron from Merthyr Tydfil to Cardiff. This was linked up with the famous canal and tramway built by Dr Richard Griffiths used to transport coal from the Rhondda Valleys.

In the 1860s Dr William Price owned some of the land in this area. Among many other roles he was employed as a physician at the Brown Lennox Chainworks near Pontypridd. Widely perceived as an eccentric in his time, he was a surgeon, political and social reformer, archdruid, as well as a pioneer of the legalisation of cremation in the United Kingdom. He left a legacy as a result of which the first crematorium in Wales was built at Glyntaff, Rhydyfelin.

Today, Rhydyfelin is probably best known as one of the stops on the Taf Trail that runs for 55 miles from Brecon in the north to Cardiff Bay in the south. This is a popular track created for cyclists and walkers. It boasts of many nature trails with beautiful vistas.

However, Rhydyfelin tends to be overshadowed by its better-known neighbours, Pontypridd and Treforest. The latter has become well known for its busy industrial estate as well as being home to the University of Glamorgan. Pontypridd and Treforest are frequently mentioned in association with the singer Tom Jones who was born and brought up in this area. According to the 2001 census, the wards of Rhydyfelin had a population of 4,652, in comparison with around 30,000 in Pontypridd as a whole.

As a result of the study done by the Bridges Project, mentioned in Chapter 2, the organisation now known as Valleys Kids was brought in here during 1997, to take part in what has now become known as the Rhydyfelin Regeneration Partnership. Social services and health visitors invited Valleys Kids to coordinate the development of youth provision in the area. Also, it helped synchronise the services created to improve the health and well being of young children, young people and families in Rhydyfelin and neighbouring Hawthorn.

In contrast to the other areas that accommodate Valleys Kids centres, there are signs of a greater social divide here. A wider range of income is evident within the Rhydyfelin area. In nearby Hawthorn several residents live in more expensive houses than can generally be found in the Rhondda. Further up the very steep hill in the Rhydyfelin vicinity, some very large housing estates have been built, which have been of poor quality, historically. At the summit, this includes the Glyntaff Farm estate which houses the Ilan centre where the Valleys Kids project was originally located. According to members of staff working there, *'a community has been created within a community – there is an up top and a down bottom.'* The hill has created a barrier between streets and neighbourhoods. Within a few hundred yards there is division between the estates on the

One of the girls I met who was involved in Youth Theatre as well as the youth club felt very strongly that had she not been caught up in these activities she would have been 'pulled down with her friends into drinking and using drugs.'

hillside. This invisible obstacle has created problems within Rhydyfelin. Dave Adamson of the University of Glamorgan reports in a Needs Assessment in 2000. *'The strong sense of localism and territoriality prevents young people travelling between existing facilities.'*

In the past, young people in the Glyntaff Farm estate (where this project was originally located) have been labelled as troublesome and antisocial. The same Needs Assessment noted above contains records of *'alcohol abuse in young children which appear routinised and normalised in the local culture.'* Members of staff feel that this image has been gradually changing for the positive, through intervention from several organisations but also largely because of the informal intergenerational community developmental work in which the Rhydyfelin Community Project has been involved. One of the girls I met who was involved in Youth Theatre as well as the youth club felt very strongly that had she not been caught up in these activities she would have been *'pulled down with her friends into drinking and using drugs.'* Today, Valleys Kids is in the process of doing more research into the drinking habits of the young in all of its areas with the purpose of trying to find more solutions.

In order to deal with these issues it has been necessary for the staff of the Rhydyfelin Project to build slowly informal and supportive relationships with the young people and families living in the area. Having done most of their work within the community at the top of the hill in the Ilan project, the team are now reaching out more to young people and families living further down.

'I can be myself here.
You don't have to
be so careful with
what you say here.
With social services,
I am careful with my
words.'

REACHING OUT TO THE WIDER COMMUNITY

One of Valleys Kids' most valuable tools has come from its ability to place itself right in the core of the community in which it serves. From the perspective of those I interviewed, this is true of the Rhydyfelin Community Project, too. Along with a commitment to support vulnerable groups, those aforementioned deep roots create many links to people who struggle with accessing statutory provision. While providing essential services, the easier more relaxed approach of a community development organisation like this means that it attracts both adults and children who have negative associations with such organisations as Children's Services, Police or Education. Working in partnership with these establishments in areas where there is a high level of poverty, Valleys Kids often acts as a bridge. It is able to stay detached from the local people's fear and the resulting stigma projected on to statutory institutions. Most of the professional staff are valleys' people which makes trust much easier in close communities like this. One mum summed up her relationship with the project. *'I can be myself here. You don't have to be so careful with what you say here. With social services, I am careful with my words.'*

Because of the aforementioned invisible barrier between the different estates on the hill and unlike the other Valleys Kids' areas where there is a community centre placed within easy reach of the neighbourhood, Rhydyfelin Community Project has decided to broaden its scope and reach out further into the vicinity it serves. Being based for a number of years in the Ilan centre at the top of the hill allowed the staff to work creatively with different groups nearby. However, the geography of the area meant that those lower down were not being reached sufficiently. In responding to the needs and demands of the community, the Rhydyfelin project is working in varied venues in different parts of the district such as a church hall, a school, the Communities First house and a flat belonging to a local housing association – as well as in the Ilan centre. Alongside this evolving expansion, the youth workers are developing more outreach work with young people, meeting them in their patch, slowly establishing contact and building trust.

Therefore, the special relationship is extended to a wider group of people. In order to understand further the nature of Valleys Kids work it is important to stop and contemplate the methods and level of engagement in this innovative community support system.

A PROFESSIONAL FRIENDSHIP

Here He Comes

Here he comes, smiling, chatty, cheeky
Alright boys, set up the pool table.
Any chance of a cup of tea?
Still smiling, still chatty, dancing around
Teasing the girls, needing to show off
Playfully goes over to the bin
Sits in, stuck!
Arms and legs flailing about
Picture – On all fours like a snail with a home on his back
Picture – A young man with the weight of the world on his shoulders.

Here he comes, not smiling, glowering, not a word
Hovers, looks around the room, kicks over the bin
Litter strewn like confetti.
Pick it up please?

No answer.
Pick it up please?
No answer.

Dark clouds gathering, storm brewing
What to do?
Close all doors and windows
Put up shutters, lock it out?
Decision – ride the storm
See it through
Wait for the sunshine.

Here he comes, smiling, cheeky, chatty
A little bit tipsy
Smartly dressed
Girl on his arm
Money in his pocket
Happy to be back, needing to show off.
Goes away, smiling, cheeky, chatty
A little bit tipsy, satisfied.
Storm has passed, sun shines through.

As written by Erika Taylor, Valleys Kids Coordinator, Rhydyfelin Community Project.

This poem encapsulates the fundamental nature of Valleys Kids' approach to interacting with all people, especially the young. It puts in a nutshell the essence of youth and community work. That is, creating a tolerant atmosphere while being aware of different moods; accepting but not overlooking certain behaviours; supporting youngsters while they work through the many difficult issues of moving into adulthood; listening on so many different levels: not just hearing the words. Above all, it requires having the right kind of relationship to understand what is needed and how best to respond.

As in all of the Valleys Kids' centres, the liaison formed between the worker and the people they are engaged with is much more informal and less defined than that of a teacher or social worker. Based on reciprocity, this relationship is established on a voluntary basis. The great majority who attend have chosen to take part in the activities provided by the project. Within the loosely structured programme of the different clubs, the depth and time of their involvement is flexible. They can come and go as they please. While staff have the final say in management decisions, the role of a youth or community worker is to stand back more, listening to the conversation in the groups; occasionally tweaking what is being discussed by opening up a new avenue of thought and making suggestions; facilitating from within.

The rapport that a youth and community worker forms with whom they work is contained within professional boundaries, within the ethos of the organisation. However, the approach is more 'Lets find the answers together.' It is more equal. It is not about telling them what they should be doing but encouraging them to find the solutions within themselves.

Kerry Young who wrote The Art of Youth Work concludes: The youth work relationship is one in which the young person is accepted and valued; the youth worker has faith in the young person; shows concern and empathy; and takes account of their experiences, opinions and ideas.'

However, there is an expectation that members are expected to honour; that is, respect for people and equipment. The young people know that there is a line that they are expected not to cross, a boundary in which behaviour is contained. It is based on a 2-way consideration for others, a fundamental trust that most

individuals have the capacity to take responsibility for their own issues, to make their own decisions, to learn from their own mistakes.

LEARNING EXPERIENCES

The 2 young women quoted at the beginning of this chapter shared examples of their experience and involvement. On the very first evening of their attendance, they were in a group of about 10 who turned up having consumed a fair amount of alcohol. *'We weren't drunk but had had enough for the staff to notice!'* They were refused entrance for that evening and a lesson was learned about crossing boundaries. A limit had been set, establishing respect. It was the beginning of a long relationship with the centre. It was where they met, formed continuing friendships and along with volunteers and staff, supported each other through their different problems over a period of 3 or 4 years (including bereavement over the death of a close friend.)

As well as the informal chats, they were involved in many of the activities of the centre. Among their memories they recalled that they took part in a dance group and drama workshops with the ArtWorks team. They had weekends away to Little Bryn Gwyn (Valleys Kids residential house in the Gower). Along with people from the Penyrenglyn Project, they formed an exchange with a group from Scotland, sharing their understandings of the different cultures. The knowledge and relationships that grew from all of these activities stay fresh in their minds.

Kayleigh was inspired by what she experienced in the centre, went on to study at university, attained a degree in youth and community work and now works as an

Educational Key Worker with kids who have difficulty in coping with mainstream school. The other young woman has gained qualifications in hotel management and catering. She had just returned from travelling, working in Australia and parts of Asia. Both see their involvement here in the project as having helped to shape the way their careers and lives are developing. It should be noted that these achievements have been reached in an area where a high number of school leavers are economically inactive and *'the performance of our young people in GCSE and equivalent examinations is below the Welsh Average'*. This quote is taken from Live Grow Aspire Achieve, Rhondda Cynon Taff's Community Strategy 2010 – 2020.

Valleys Kids youth and community worker, Nicola highlighted a recent learning experience for another group of young people. As well as working informally with young people and families she develops workshops with them helping to tackle existing concerns in their lives. Issues such as alcohol, drugs, and sexual health have been addressed in this way. At the time of our conversation, among many other undertakings, she had been working with three 15 year old girls caught bullying another outside the youth club. Although they apologised to the victim, Nicola asked those responsible to think about what action she should take with them. Their considered reply was that they should be banned. In this instance, further conversation decided that they would be banned for 2 weeks and take part in a workshop on bullying. Initially, only the 3 girls would participate in this but they would be expected to take this peer-led workshop to the wider club, helping them to consider the different forms of intimidation, how it makes other people feel and what leads people to behaving this way. If their behaviour improved no further action would be taken. If the bullying continued parents would then be contacted.

In these surroundings, learning comes from new and different experiences; from trying new approaches; from bonding with others; from having adventures; from making mistakes and gaining wisdom through that process.

In these surroundings, learning comes from new and different experiences; from trying new approaches; from bonding with others; from having adventures; from making mistakes and gaining wisdom through that process.

DARING TO BE ADVENTUROUS

In discussion here, the team expressed a concern about modern societies' institutionalisation of people - particularly the young. While recognising the need for and the importance of the structure of the more formal social organisations, they pointed out that over the years spontaneity of the young has been hampered. There had always been street play in this area, historically. Gradually, because of the volume of today's traffic, health and safety concerns and the general fear of adults, this is being taken away. A void has been created where fun and risk-taking have little importance. The staff see the Rhydyfelin Community Project as rising to fill that gap: providing a safe space where children can work out the kind of relationships formed in bygone years when they were allowed to be more adventurous, to explore their environment, to learn from nature.

I visited a fairly new Afterschools Club in the Communities First House, halfway up the hill and talked to the young participants. Among others, Anne- Marie (aged 10), twins Oliver and Natalia (8) and Devon (5) were in the process of making blueberry pancakes, under supervision. I enquired what they liked about the club. They were animated as they chatted about their exciting activities. They were quick to tell me that it was fun, that they get to play and to try different activities.

What had been most exciting for them were the experiences of creating fire-porridge and learning bush-craft skills in the forest. Beautiful patterns were created when the fire-porridge was lit. (This was made from a mixture of sand, paraffin and sawdust). This supervised workshop was geared to help young people treat fire with respect. During the introduction to bush-craft skills, the twins were thrilled by being taught how to recognise the difference between an acorn nibbled by a squirrel and another chewed by mice! An experience denied to many modern, more restricted young people.

LONG TERM RELATIONSHIPS

Nicola reflected on the importance of establishing early contact with the younger children. The Afterschools Clubs present an opportunity for providing play and they also create an opening to start building long-term relationships. Over a period of several years many children progress through different groups and activities. As a result, by the time these children are old enough to attend the youth club, trust and respect has already been well established. With teenagers a time-honoured rapport can be a great advantage. A respectful base has been formed from which people can learn and grow. She commented *'I wouldn't want to work with kids I hadn't formed a relationship with.'* She defines her role as informally maintaining relationships with young people, making sure she is there for them so that she can support them with any issues or problems they might want to talk about. Those supportive interactions can go through many cycles. Having worked for Valleys Kids for 12 years, one of her original afterschools' kids is now bringing her baby to a parent and toddler group, which is facilitated by Nicola.

Often these contacts are established through relaxed activities. Nathan, another youth worker at the Rhydyfelin Community Project and his colleague Victoria, a play worker, discussed the time it took to establish these informal relationships and how long it can take for people of all ages to adapt and learn to trust their own innate abilities. They saw some local people as being more familiar and perhaps more comfortable with the structure of the statutory organisations, dependent on the people in authority for making decisions, telling them what to do. Nathan described his approach to a group of young people attempting some artwork. He saw his role as *showing them the basics and letting them get on with it*, finding their own way of developing the work and learning by experience. There is no pressure to produce a conventionally acceptable neat and tidy picture. Initially, youngsters struggled with that freedom of expression but gradually self-confidence has grown as they have learned to trust their own skills and communicate their own individuality.

A NETWORK OF SUPPORT

Adults benefit from the support given here, too. Glenys, Zoë, Amanda, Julie, and Mandy are all attending the Rhydyfelin Women's Group, which is part of the community project. Aged between 27 and 68 years, they all come together once a week to *blurt it all out*. Having a laugh was clearly high on the agenda but the main purpose of meeting in the group is to have a break from the stresses of family life. It is a mutual support group and clearly is very important to each of them. One woman was returning to work but her hours had been arranged around still being able to attend on a Friday. Through meeting for coffee and taking part in different activities that they choose, close friendships have been formed. All have each other's

'It helps me stand up and be counted. I'm more assertive with rude people. Coming here has built my confidence.'

telephone numbers so that they could call or meet up if the community workers were unable to be there.

Three of the women summed up their reason for turning out.

'It helps me stand up and be counted. I'm more assertive with rude people. Coming here has built my confidence.'

'When I am listening to other people's problems, I feel easier. When I am sitting alone in the house I begin to think that I am the only one who feels this way. It helps me to know that other people have got problems too.'

I've always been wrapped up in my family. This is the first time I have had time just for myself.'

When asked about the goals of the Rhydyfelin Community Project, the staff team clearly saw one of their main aims as building up relationships with kids and families with the purpose of bringing the community together. Many of the conversations with youth and community workers as well as local people emphasised the importance of cooperation, the gradual building up of trust. For example, the afterschool club in Rhydyfelin opens up opportunities for different age groups, with parents coming along as volunteers. While the mums' and dads' main intention is to help with homework, they also find support for themselves. Gradually, they jell together as a group in the process of getting to know the other adults, helping bring the community closer together. Also, as the volunteers become more involved in the activities of the centre they start to see a different side to young people. The different generations begin to listen to each other. Adults lose the fear of youth, appreciating that they are *'not all bad.'* The young become less withdrawn, more outgoing. Communication increases

*A place where
people feel safe,
comforted, accepted,
heard, supported,
encouraged to
feel good about
themselves and to
expand their lives.
A neighbourhood
where dividing lines
can be diminished
over time.*

and relationships across the age groups start to form, improving the spirit of community.

The importance of intergenerational relationships is developed in further chapters. Also, we will look at some of the partnerships that Valleys Kids shares with the statutory organisations and how that co-operation benefits young people and their families.

In the meantime, the lesson to be learned from the people of the Rhydyfelin Community Project (as well as the other centres mentioned in this book) is the necessity for such an initiative rooted in the heart of a community. A place where people feel safe, comforted, accepted, heard, supported, encouraged to feel good about themselves and to expand their lives. A neighbourhood where dividing lines can be diminished over time. That message came through clearly from all of the people in every age group that I interviewed.

It is essential to acknowledge the special skills it takes to create that atmosphere – that is, the ability to generate the kind of relationship that develops a mutual trust, the fundamental basis for change.

CHAPTER 5

Finding out about Pen Dinas Community Project

'The project has made a difference to the kids. The kids have got different attitudes. The kids are changing; that means the adults have to change, too.'

Rob made this statement. He has been a resident of Pen Dinas for 5 years and is stepfather to some young people who have attended this project. Perhaps he has not always been the greatest fan of some of the young on the estate but he has observed their more positive outlook and enjoys the effect it has on the community's way of thinking and responding. What he was describing is a growing feeling of hope that life might be improving, along with a tentative stirring of belief that the residents have the right to deserve these changes.

At the time of writing this, the buildings of Pen Dinas are undergoing a long awaited and much deserved external upgrading and makeover. Like all of the community projects that come under the Valleys Kids umbrella, this area has had a difficult history. At last, it appears that positive change is happening for the people who live there.

A STARTING POINT

Pen Dinas is a group of 66 flats contained in 5 blocks within the district of Dinas, a section of the ward of Porth.

A ribbon development, it is bounded by Penygraig and a very busy main road to the south, with the River Rhondda and parallel railway line enclosing it to the north. The flats are within easy walking distance of the railway station. Trealaw is the neighbouring village beyond the railway.

The homes are built close to the former pitheads of the Dinas collieries. Dinas lower colliery is believed to be the first mining shaft to have been sunk in the Rhondda.

Once a close mining village with the usual pub, chapel, farm, pithead and houses, Dinas has become an enclave in more recent years with no particular affiliations to any other community. A number of the older buildings were demolished and replaced by housing estates in the 1960s and 70s. Neighbourhoods within Dinas itself have little to do with each other, the residents and young people in particular being quite territorial. Having lost the dynamics of a formed village, it has become more of a drive through area. Despite having a poor health record and because it is part of the Porth ward it is not seen as eligible for Communities First funding although it would benefit greatly from it. It is the only one of the Valleys Kids projects that does not qualify for this support. Porth is viewed as one of the better off communities in the Rhondda, relatively speaking. This assessment denies that although the greater population of this area enjoys a healthier lifestyle, there are pockets within the neighbourhood where families are not able to share in that comparatively comfortable way of life.

A feasibility study on Dinas prepared by Katherine Hughes Associates in 2003 describes the outside of the flats: *'The environment to the rear of the flats is poor: it seems that the intended use of the area was for car parking, although even now car ownership is very low. Because of car crime, poor lighting and vandalism to the garages, the*

area to the back of the flats is seldom used for residents' parking. Instead residents park on the main road at the front. Boundary chain fencing for some of the small plots has been broken in places; the area is unsuitable and not used for play. The playground at the top of the block has lost most of its equipment.' Over the years, visitors to the community project, used to a more cared-for way of life have expressed shock at the condition of this area; in particular at the feeling of oppression caused by the neglect of the appearance of the buildings and the immediate environment.

This description also states: 'There is a small core of older residents who moved into their flats when they were built (in the late 60s/ early 70s) who are committed to stay. However, overall there is a high turnover in the flats. Often they are used as a stop-gap before moving elsewhere.'

Through the Eyes of Children, an assessment written in the same year by Jo Olney, Valleys Kids community development worker, and Liz Cutland, then community family worker, asks the question: *'What makes life difficult in Pen Dinas?'* Among other concerns, the reply was, *'A lack of local shops and facilities; poor environmental issues; joy riders (usually from outside the estate) dumping cars down the bank and setting fire to them; unsafe areas for kids to play; fighting against a poor reputation; feeling ignored by supporting services; visitors to the area, as well as some neighbours disrespecting the surroundings and the rights of the residents; poverty traps; financial disabilities; and the frustration of not being listened to.'*

This last report remarks on a pervading sense of defeat, at that time. It notes that Pen Dinas was a prime example of how many years of oppression and negativity could hamper or destroy the foundations of community interaction, creating a wall of depression and suspicion.

LIFTING THE ATMOSPHERE

Valleys Kids became involved in the area after Sure Start had made some inroads there. In Pen Dinas, Sure Start had recognised the needs of 0 to 4 years olds, as well as those of their families. Flat 54 became the centre of developing such support during the year 2000. Many ideas were formed during the 18 months of their stay and Sure Start identified that the requirements of the community far outstretched their remit of working with 4 years old and under. However, it became apparent to them that cliques had emerged, dividing the population of the neighbourhood. As a result of the friction in the community, attendance of the little ones and their families shrunk. Fewer children could be helped.

Centred in flat 54 since 2002, Valleys Kids, with Jo Olney as the original community development worker, has been able to offer the community a range of services and support. Jo was an artist and held the belief that *'positivity led to creativity'*. One of the first ventures that she introduced to engage the children and to help raise spirits was an art project. The young people all drew life-sized outlines of themselves on plywood, cutting them out and colouring them brightly. For many years, on a drive south from the Rhondda Fawr, Pen Dinas caught the eye of the passers-by. Valleys Kids and Rhondda Housing helped the children of the community stamp their claim on their home area by erecting these impressive images on the exposed gable wall of the end block of flats. That symbolic gesture was the start of many projects that helped improve the image and spirit of the community, slowly.

Over the years, environmental work gradually helped make the surrounds more child-friendly. Adults and young people in particular have been involved in litter picking in environment. In the early days Andrew Hopkins who was community advocate often helped them. At that time to keep the immediate area safe for children to play, Jo regularly gathered abandoned needles from heroin syringes. Also, she worked together with Keep Wales Tidy encouraging young residents to help clean up the river. She engaged with Arriva trains. As a result, Dinas station enjoyed a tidy up, too. A fenced-in play area around flat 54 was created, complete with sensory garden. Her successor, Nicola Davies also worked hard with the young people gradually encouraging them to take some responsibility in improving the surrounding area. While doing this, she persuaded them to try different experiences away from Pen Dinas and the Rhondda. Among other activities, she took many of them camping, canoeing and kayaking.

During her time there, the most challenging and uplifting project came in 2006 when H.R.H. Prince William visited the flats through contact with another project in Valleys Kids. For this visit, the community came together to help improve the appearance of the buildings and surrounding area. To the benefit of those that used the premises, Flat 54 was given a makeover for that event: the area around the flats and the walk along the river were tidied up. Rob, who had just moved to Pen Dinas said: *'I knew then that this place had something special. No other community like ours in the Rhondda had Prince William visiting them.'*

Since then RCT Homes and Connaught have extended the premises at Flat 54, creating new offices there for admin and quiet, confidential discussions, as well as an area for a new snooker table and other activities. RCT Homes is also responsible for the long-awaited and ongoing upgrading of all of the buildings.

A RAY OF HOPE

It has been a number of years since a joy rider has dumped a stolen car in Pen Dinas and set fire to it. It has been about the same length of time since a heroin needle has been picked up in the grounds. Change of attitude has happened definitely: progressively, if tentatively.

During recent visits, as someone who was quite closely involved in the earlier days of Valleys Kids' participation in Pen Dinas, I was struck by the change of atmosphere brought about by the improvements to the fabric of the buildings. At the time of writing this, the estate is a building site and is likely to be so for about 18 months. However, adults were almost allowing themselves to believe that life and their environs could be improving but they were not quite ready to trust that their luck was in – just yet. Although a huge amount of money is being spent on a new roof on each building with new felting and a solar heating system; although new security doors are in place making the buildings feel safer; although the smelly, unhygienic rubbish chutes have been removed; although the community has been consulted on further improvements the attitude is still, 'We will see.' There is a cautious atmosphere of hope but it will still take years before communities like this trust that they are seen as worthy of good things occurring. They have been more used to 'the crap that happens.'

Roger, who is the present community development worker in Pen Dinas sees this physical improvement as great positive progress contributing to the uplifting of the community. However, he believes that what is needed now is continued *'spiritual change'*. His aim is to help move Pen Dinas forward, to encourage those living there to see that being a more cohesive community would change their lives considerably. This would give them the power to change their circumstances even more, if they wanted to. He hopes that there will be a return to the old neighbourhood values of the mining period when communities were more united and supportive of each other.

At this time, Eileen, Valleys Kids play and family worker on the estate sees a core in the community who help hold it together. In the period of just under the 4 years she has worked there she has experienced residents gradually getting on better with each other. Some new families have moved in and jelled; others stay on the periphery of the community keeping a watchful distance while a few have chosen to move on, again. There is hope that the improvement of the fabric of the buildings along with the continuing support for children and families will change that, making it easier for new residents to accept and be accepted; increasing the stability of the neighbourhood.

Recently, more adults have become involved in flat 54, using it as a drop-in centre, having a cup of tea, and sometimes talking about their problems, finding out where they can get help with different issues. Over the years the community has come together for different events. Last Christmas, the elderly were invited by the young for a meal. When I was visiting, they were making plans to have a street party for the Royal Wedding, also.

A mum who has recently returned to live in Pen Dinas with her son found that volunteering at the centre helped her settle into the community. Helping the staff work with the youngsters in the middle youth club gave her a sense of belonging. That is what a number of people of all ages find as they become drawn into the project, an encouragement to become involved in taking joint responsibility for the improvement of the neighbourhood. Perhaps in that commitment to good citizenship they find a way of fitting in, planting some roots in the area.

MAKING LIFE BETTER FOR CHILDREN

In keeping with Valleys Kids' aim to help improve the
quality of life for the young, different activities in Pen Dinas
have been developed with that purpose in mind.

Funding gained from the Big Lottery for a period of 3
years through a scheme called Fresh Beginnings made
a difference to what could be achieved with little ones
who live here. Valleys Kids used this financial support for
introducing new activities and new experiences, along with
exercise and food. This scheme was aimed at trying to get
kids away from their televisions for a while; getting them
out and about. Activities were created to include travelling
away from home. Central to these were picnics with lots
of fresh foods and salads. Through these trips, youngsters
have learned that they can choose to eat different kinds
of fruit instead of something else. Further development of
that theme of healthy eating means that a cookery club has
been introduced in the community flat so that mums can
learn to cook on a budget. The cooking class is run by one
of the residents, one of the Dads.

Eileen has witnessed that the availability of this money has
created a huge impact. She described one child who at four
and a half years had been seen as extremely withdrawn,
refusing to speak. Now 6 years old, she has become more
confident, more outward going and among other activities,
attends a drama group with great enthusiasm. Being able
to get out of the area on such occasions has expanded her
experience and helped lift her confidence. Through the Pen
Dinas Community project, Valleys Kids has helped widen
her horizons, even at this very early age.

Days away are very special and important to these young
people. Pen Dinas may be built next to a railway station

and on a regular bus route but if families have little money, it is impossible to make use of those facilities. Projects like this create opportunities. Otherwise, the children rarely have the chance to go anywhere. Their experience of life is restricted to their home area.

YOUNG PEOPLE MAKING LIFE BETTER FOR THEMSELVES

Through commitment and hard work, the staff and volunteers of Valleys Kids have helped effect change for young people and their families in Pen Dinas. It also has to be acknowledged and recorded that some change is happening in this housing estate because of the youngsters who live there.

The children and young people of Pen Dinas are aware that they live on an estate that has a poor reputation. They know that unfair judgement reflects on them and wonder why people think negatively of them. Despite having to deal with that local prejudice and despite some of them coming from families who have difficulties, several of those in their late teens have held their head high, formed their own aspirations and aimed for them.

I met with 3 young people: Chris aged 16, Donna on her 19th birthday and Sarah who was 17. All had been involved with the project for 8 or 9 years and talked about it with much enthusiasm. In the face of the powerful effects of the recession and regardless of the valleys' history of some unemployment spanning 3 generations, all were pursuing their intended careers with great eagerness. Chris was training to be a chef and if he passes his exams has been offered a job in a well-known chain of restaurants. Donna, who was aware and proud of her *'good organisational skills'*, is a clerical assistant in the NHS, currently working with dieticians and has ambitions to develop her skills and further her career. Sarah has stayed on in school and gained an NVQ in childcare. Regardless of living in an area where there is high unemployment and it is difficult to find work, all three appeared to have clear pictures of what they wanted to achieve and have stepped on the first rung of the career ladder. Other young people in the group appeared busy, involved in different training courses, hoping that work will appear for them.

It is hard in this financial climate with some youngsters applying for over 100 jobs before they even get an interview. A challenge for communities struggling in the long and slow process of recovery from the closure of the pits is how they keep this raw enthusiasm for betterment alive during a modern and continued recession with poor employment prospects.

In 2010, the Princes Trust reported that the number of young people in unemployment in Wales was at a 12 year high. A later study (The Princes Trust Youth Index) published in 2013 highlights the impact of unemployment on people between the ages of 16 and 25. Those nationwide results included:

- **1 in 10 young people feel unable to cope with life. Those in unemployment are more than twice as likely to feel unable to cope than their peers.**
- **More than 1 in 5 young people feel they have no future due to the recession.**
- **More than 1 in 5 young people did not have someone to talk to about their problems when growing up.**

'The centre is not just a place to go and have fun it is also a place that makes you feel safe.'

It begs many questions. How do many young people survive if they do not have a local support service like the one in Pen Dinas? Where do they go for help when the governmental system has let them down so badly? What message are we giving them about their importance and their future? What legacy are we leaving them?

The 3 young people who I interviewed were very articulate on what their involvement in the Pen Dinas project had done for them. As in other areas, when asked what impact the projects have had on their lives, the greatest majority replied: *'It has been somewhere for me to go. It has kept me off the streets.'* When probed further about why that is important, the response was spontaneous, unanimous and somewhat surprised that I needed to ask this question. *' Because I would be like my friends who don't go to a place like this – getting into trouble with drugs and booze. There is nothing else to do.'* Chris wrote a testament for one of the funders of the project. This included the statement: *'The centre is not just a place to go and have fun it is also a place that makes you feel safe.'* He shared that it was where he could go and talk about his problems and when he did so *'they just seemed to disappear.'* Donna echoed the importance of knowing this was where she could come for support if she needed it.

Donna had moved out of Pen Dinas but still kept up regular attendance at the project. She returns to visit her grandmother and to socialise with her friends. She appreciated being involved in the decision making process of the Youth Club. *'It makes us feel important.'* Being made aware of the budgets and what they could afford to spend, they were involved in choosing colour schemes for the flat. Also, they were encouraged to decide on different activities in which they wanted to be involved. The most recent plans concern a trip to Snowdonia. *'We are discussing how we do it and how do we raise the money.'* Often called to get the group working together, she obviously enjoyed the staff and friends valuing her ability to get things done.

Sarah appreciated that her involvement with the project meant, *'I have done things I would never have done.'* By this, she meant taking part in different activities like kayaking, canoeing, mountain biking and raft-building. While these activities were adventurous and great fun for them all, Chris pointed out that he now realized that he had learned good skills in the process. *'Take raft building for example. You learn to work as a team. You also learn to use the things you've got to make something.'*

DEVELOPING TEAMWORK

It seems that within the senior youth group, team work *'is something that happens a lot here.'* The support of the peers and working together in groups was considered important particularly in relation to continuing the physical improvement of the estate. Teamwork brought the groups of friends from the estate and nearby more closely together. It is a constructive method of listening to different thoughts and opinions, planning different activities together, valuing each other's skills and supporting each other through the hard times – as well as expending energy and having fun together.

Among the young, the attitude about the upgrading was less reserved than that of some of the adults. Their enthusiasm is less cautious. *'I can tell it is going to be much different,'* said Sarah. Continuing the improvement of Pen Dinas was seen as requiring a lot of hard work and togetherness to make it happen, keep it tidy. Donna felt they should all take more care – not just those who come to *'youth.'* She was hoping that the wider community would get more involved in the energy and teamwork of continuing to upgrade the atmosphere and environment. Indeed, that may happen. There are some early signs that a tenants and residents association is on the cards.

The experience of Pen Dinas helps to highlight the fact that the recovery of the old mining communities is a very gradual process that can take decades. It also assists us in realising that the slow healing from poverty is twofold: both physical and spiritual and the two are interdependent. You cannot have one without the other. At long last, both these roads seem to becoming together in Pen Dinas. Availability of work would make the picture complete for many, lifting individual and collective esteem. However, the buildings are being improved and with the development of a community heart and much nurturing of the community spirit, hope for the future is now more than a mere flicker.

One of the mums commented. *'People can stop criticising us now.'*

Chris summed up the influence of the changes. *'This is where we start to take over. It is our home and we need to be proud of it.'*

CHAPTER 6

Catching up with the Penygraig Community Project

'This place proves that the generations can mix. We can all learn from each other. The young teach us about technology. They learn about life experiences from us. Before, the older ones thought that the children were rude. They thought people from the older generation were dirty and smelly.'

This comment came from Pat who is a woman in her 60s. Very active as a volunteer in the project, she runs a bingo club for the older people helping them be less isolated in their homes. She is also chairperson for the steering group committee of Penygraig and District Communities First. Interested in improving relationships between young and old, she cooks with the kids aged around 13 and14 on a Saturday, helps out with summer playschemes and has been involved in producing intergenerational shows with them. She has taken part in the Mzansi Cymru Choir, part of Valleys Kids and the Wales' Cultural Olympiad, which includes people of all ages.

Pat's comments along with other shared experiences in this chapter underline the importance of relationship between different age groups, creating an atmosphere of mutual support. She follows Marion who (as well as being

a member of 'the older generation' and a trustee of Valleys Kids) has been a volunteer working with the young since she was widowed several years ago.

Youth work in Valleys Kids is not isolated from the rest of the community as it can be in other organisations. The greatest emphasis of the organisation is for the young to have time on their own, socialising with their peers - under supervision of qualified youth workers and volunteers from the community. Yet it is recognized that people of all ages have much to offer each other. Here, the different generations are learning to integrate to the benefit of all.

THE NEW ROOTED IN THE OLD

First, in order to appreciate the mood of the present day, we must understand a little of the geography and history of the village of Penygraig. Near Tonypandy in the Rhondda Fawr, Penygraig was recorded as having a population of 5,877 in the 2001 census. Coalmining began here in 1857 and over the years the area suffered from several fatal disasters particularly in the Ely Colliery, part of the Cambrian Combine owned by Viscount Rhondda.

The hub of Valleys Kids at 1 Cross Street, Penygraig is based in what had been the head office of the once very successful Penygraig Industrial Co-operative Society set up in 1891. It was during the bitter Cambrian Colliery dispute (1910-1911) that the benefits of the Cooperative Society were really shown. At the beginning of the tensions the Co-op granted the striking members 15 shillings per week to ease the families hardship and the Society supplied provisions at cost price to the miners' committee for soup kitchens, according to the Rhondda Cynon Taf Heritage Trail (online). The Co-operative Society also played a social, cultural and educational role in the community. Classes were made available to members and members' children; choirs were formed, concerts and eisteddfods organised, educational grants offered and lectures and films shown. It was a vital centre of the community in Penygraig where people made dividend and share capital withdrawals, collected tickets for hospital treatment and made savings bank deposits.

The placing of the community project in Penygraig shows how Valleys Kids is deeply anchored in the traditions and history of the area. Penygraig Community Centre itself is based in Soar Ffrwdamos, which was built in 1832 as one of the first Baptist chapels in the Rhondda. Part of the building was donated by the congregation in 1978 and has undergone 2 renovation programmes since then. It is now a state-of-the-art community centre. These days, a building of this quality is more likely to be seen in Cardiff rather than the valleys. Seen by many as the centre of the local area, it lifts the atmosphere of the surrounding village, which enjoyed better years during the success of the mining industry.

These buildings were first erected in a time of relative prosperity, which was followed by a sharp decline as the collieries closed leaving families and communities in dire straits. The crisis of today is not quite so acute but the after-effects of history linger on and mingle with 21st century recession. Valleys Kids carries on the practice that originated in these buildings: supporting families and helping people to improve their lives. Those values of the mining communities, those original ideals of the Penygraig Community Projects are what links the past with the present and continue to provide strength and stability to many.

MOVING INTO THE 21ST CENTURY

The Bike Club (as local people call it) or Soar as the building is officially named has been transformed into a modern and attractive community centre. When Pat first started coming with her sisters to see different shows produced there the beauty of the building amazed her. Now, she is pleased to see it being used by the older generation as well as the younger age groups.

The interior of the building has changed greatly and the outside has enjoyed an eye-catching upgrade too, although a passer by would still recognise its origins as a typical valleys' chapel. Valleys Kids now owns both floors of the building as well as the vestry. (The small congregation of Soar Chapel continue to meet in that well-used space towards the back of the building.) The upper floor of the building has been converted into a theatre where many drama productions and larger community events take place.

In 2005, the building was closed in order for the renovations to progress. Rhodri Morgan, the First Minister, reopened it in 2006. In this same year, further money was secured for renovating the vestry.

This interim period was a time of adaptation, of innovation, of working with groups of young people and adults in a restricted place. In true Valleys Kids' fashion, in limited circumstances the staff and young people modified their activities well. The numbers attending did drop but the staff and volunteers believe that this was a time when they were able to develop closer relationships while doing good quality youthwork with small groups. The young peoples' imaginations were challenged. They were creative in their fun and activities. They were resilient and adjusted, playing

As the flagship of the organisation, Soar attracts large numbers and the challenge is to balance all the demands of the community.

football in the rain and transforming some of the plentiful supply of scaffolding into a climbing frame.

The opening of the new building brought a time of change and refreshment. While anchored in the values of the past, it brought an opportunity to reassess, to keep what had worked well in earlier times and to alter some attitudes that had become outdated. This process of adapting to change developed as an even wider approach to community development work evolved.

BALANCING THE NEEDS OF THE COMMUNITY

Change brings new issues to face. The earlier Bike Club's aim was to help improve the futures of the young people and families in the community – to help them help themselves. That ambition is engrained in Valleys Kids methodology and continues to this day. However, the size and pleasant appearance of the building, the way the floors have been planned, the demands on the modern theatre have made it possible to open its doors to many other people. As in most of the areas it serves and as it has moved forward in time, Valleys Kids has widened its arms even further, welcoming all age groups. As the flagship of the organisation, Soar attracts large numbers and the challenge is to balance all the demands of the community. Conversations with different people revealed some of those areas of adjustment:

- Sometimes, when a large event is taking place regular youth club evenings have to be cancelled. The young people I spoke to did not appear to be too bothered by this, taking it in their stride. However, some of the adults struggle to be as tolerant. On occasion, when different age groups share the building, the boisterous behaviour and noise of the young raises challenges for the staff who are faced with keeping the peace between the generations.

- In the past, young people were encouraged to see the centre as their own, to stamp their mark on the property by putting their pictures and other works of art on the wall. That attitude has changed with the evolution of a more modern, more all-embracing community centre. Some of those people who were members before the latest renovations tend to view this as a loss.

- The large numbers of young people attending the youth clubs worried some of the volunteers and staff. In an evening, there can be 60 to 70 youngsters attending the Senior Youth Club or 80 to a 100 of the Middle Youth Club filling the building. While being pleased that the centre is so popular and obviously meeting many needs, there was some anxiety that children from difficult backgrounds may not feel safe enough to come forward and find some support for their problems. The concern was that they might be being passed over or slipping through the net.

Gradually working together to find solutions, the staff, volunteers and different age groups are willing to rise to these challenges. On-going discussion with all concerned brings answers to balancing the universal needs with the requirements of different individuals. Children's pictures are placed on boards. As is described in later chapters, small group work is accommodated by trips to Little Bryn Gwyn, and being involved in ArtWorks and Future Families. Dialogue is encouraged prompting the different age groups to find solutions and co-operate more effectively.

The greatest feeling expressed amongst all age groups was of gratitude for having such a facility in their community. Jordan, aged 13, said very seriously that he wanted to find a way of paying Valleys Kids back for raising the money and providing such a great centre for them all. He was unaware that he is already doing that, as he is a regular volunteer helping with different arts and crafts workshops run for the younger children during holiday play schemes. Jordan is giving to - as well as benefiting from the experiences provided by the community project.

WHAT GOES AROUND COMES AROUND

Neil is someone else who gave to and benefited from his involvement with Valleys Kids. He has experienced both the earlier and present day approaches of this project. He was a member of the Bike Club in the 1980s, well involved in the activities of this time such as weightlifting, the shows produced by Denis Stallard and Pauline, football, bouncy castles and learning the basics about computers. He also has memories of being 'a naughty boy,' spraying graffiti on walls, smashing windows, being a nuisance at discos. In his younger days he was banned from the centre on several occasions.

Today, he is in his late 30s and until recently he was the caretaker/technician of Soar and a volunteer with the 5 a-side football teams. He says his recent involvement with the Bike Club has 'brought me out'. Shy, previously working on building sites, he found it hard to communicate with others. He enjoyed his work with Valleys Kids and has discovered that actually he is good with people, that folks of all ages like him. He wants to help young boys who misbehave like he did. He attributes his recently found confidence to the support he has had from staff in the Penygraig Community Centre. His colleagues Kath, Ross and Debra have all helped him gain in self-assurance and with their guidance he finds he wants to help others in return.

'It made me feel special, made me feel normal.'

Generally, this appears to be a fairly established pattern in Valleys Kids: being helped and supported by someone in the organisation, changing direction in life and wanting to pass that experience on, to reach out to others, to help make a difference.

THE IMPORTANCE OF ROLE MODELS

Separately, I met with 2 young women who wanted to continue discussing this theme about individuals from different age groups helping and supporting each other. I learned from their histories and perspectives the importance of finding someone who inspires goals to aim for.

Becky now aged 25 is close to gaining a degree in youth and community work. Chelsea, aged 16 years is a volunteer with the middle youth club. Becky used to baby-sit Chelsea when they were younger and influenced the younger women's involvement in the project.

Becky says that studying for her degree has made her realise that although there is great pressure on professionals to measure outcomes today, the effects of Youth and Community work cannot really be calculated. She went on to elaborate, *'Untold stories make it what it is. It is about how people feel, how they are inside.'* Her own story with Valleys Kids has been one of personal growth. Leaving school with no qualifications she is very surprised to find that she almost has that degree. *'When I was at school, I knew I had ability but chose not to work. I hated being there.'* Like many young people attending the projects she came from a family that had many difficulties. The Bike Club was what gave her stability and encouragement. *'It made me feel special, made me feel normal.'* Attending a playgroup at the project from when she was 2 years old (then brought by her sister), she started attending on her own, aged 6. Progressing through after-school club, middle youth club, senior youth club, she has been present there over the years (on average) about 4 times a week. She views the staff there as family and she is grateful to them for giving her that security, helping build her self-esteem and encouraging her steps forward into a career she loves. Becky was quite open about aspiring to be similar to different members of staff, viewing them as role models, wanting to reach for what they had achieved.

In turn, along with other colleagues working in Soar, Becky has influenced Chelsea among others. Chelsea is the eldest of 5 children. Her parents have separated and she carries a lot of the responsibility for looking after the younger ones in the family. Of the Bike Club she says, *'I feel welcome. I am more comfortable here than anywhere else. I feel I am part of the furniture.'*

Chelsea is in the 6th form at school but doesn't enjoy it very much, either. Well able, she considered going the academic route. However, she reassessed the situation. *'Volunteering for Valleys Kids has changed my opinion and I know you have got to work towards what you want to do.'* She acknowledges that she wants to work with people so she has started involving herself in courses on playwork and youthwork. She wants to learn more about setting up youth forums. *'The people at the Bike Club have set me on stepping stones which will guide me towards getting a job at the end.'*

STEPPING STONES

Chelsea considered why people attend the youth activities in the centre. She summed it up. *'Some come because they love it. Some people come to get out of the cold. Others come for the activities and trips. They all have different reasons.'*

As I spent time listening to different groups, it seemed to me that many of these youngsters used this facility as a stepping-stone or a road in to finding new experiences in their lives. In Soar, the building that houses the Penygraig Community Project, I met with Morgan (aged 11), Zoë (aged 13), and Jordan (also 13) from the middle youth club. Later, I also learned from the experiences of 3 older members from the senior youth club, Lauren (aged 17) another Zoë (aged 18) and Matthew (also 18 years old). All responded very positively to my questions. I asked them what benefits they found in attending the community centre. They listed several, including the following:

- Both girls named Zoë said that one of the main reasons they attended the Bike Club was to widen their circle of friends. The younger Zoë saw different people at school but it was only in the environment of the youth club that she was able to socialise with them. Zoë the elder enjoyed the chance to meet with pupils from some of the other schools in the valleys who also attended the project.
- Jordan, through his work as a volunteer, found he enjoyed working with kids and has aspirations to pursue a career doing just that. He thought that his experience at the centre would look good on his CV. Lauren, also a volunteer, teaches dance most nights of the week to some of the younger girls including Morgan and the

younger Zoë. In turn, she has opened up experiences for some of those young people in the dance team by entering them in different competitions, travelling to different places as far as North Wales to take part. One of the teams won their section of a competition, raising self-esteem.

- Trips away from home were very popular. An annual enterprise undertaken by a group of young people is to join a sponsored Bike Ride. Many of those I interviewed saw this as an adventure occurring over a period of several days taking them away from the valleys to West Wales, having a new experience.

- It was the police who introduced Matthew to the Bike Club. When he was 10 or 11, he used to *'hang about'* on a roundabout close to the centre, throwing eggs and stones at passing cars. Eventually, he took up the recommendation of the police and started attending the middle youth club. That involvement got him out of trouble. *'I have never looked back,'* he says.

- In discussion, the older group brought to the fore the initiatives that had taken place *'to teach kids right from wrong and get them to do something for the community.'* For example, members from across the age groups helped decorate the local bus shelter in order to get rid of graffiti. There is an expectation within the centre that property is treated with respect. All three felt quite strongly that the community should be given the same respectful treatment as the Bike Club.

One of the aims of Valleys Kids is to broaden horizons. These youngsters appear to be realizing that dream. That is what they were illustrating as they talked to me. In attending the different clubs their life was expanded in so many ways. It brought new friendships and support; career potential; change of lifestyle; opportunities to embrace responsibilities; an understanding of good citizenship;

'There is people respect here. Everybody is treated the same way. The underprivileged kids are treated the same. Nobody is different.'

prospects of seeing other parts of the country; exciting activities; chances to be creative; a feeling of belonging; a growing understanding between generations: a sense of achievement; higher self-esteem and a feeling of safety as they tried out some if not all of these new possibilities.

FEELING SAFE

As I wandered amongst the centres interviewing young people, this issue of feeling safe in the youth clubs kept popping up in conversation. Initially, I assumed that what they were meaning was the usual initial response. *'It keeps me off the streets. It keeps me out of trouble.'* With the older group of youth in Penygraig I probed further into this common statement. The response I was given helped me grasp that it was as I understood it AND it helped me appreciate that it was also about much more than that. The feeling of safety that the 3 young people were describing came from being respected; from being treated as equals; from being contained within clear but fair boundaries; from being listened to. This is backed up by the following comments:

'On the streets you are likely to get beaten up. In here (the Bike Club) it is not likely to happen.'

This fear seemed very real across the centres despite a Home Office report (January 2011) stating that violent crime in Rhondda Cynon Taff was down by almost 7% in the years 2009/ 2010.

'There is people respect here. Everybody is treated the same way. The underprivileged kids are treated the same. Nobody is different.'

'Kids can't be excluded. It's not like school where the teachers go for the brainier kids.'

'There are no rules as such as long as there is no vandalism. Vandalism, bullying, abusive language, drinking and violence: none of those are allowed. We know that. You would be asked to leave if you did those things.'

'My mam thinks this is a safe place for me to go and meet people. I almost live here. It's great.'

As I listened to their remarks, I was reminded of an observation from the book The Art of Youth Work written by Kerry Young. She states: 'The relationship between youth worker and young person is also underpinned by a set of essential values....

- Accepting and valuing young people
- Trust
- Honesty
- Respect
- Reciprocity.'

Clearly, these values had a large role to play in creating that atmosphere of safety. Evidently, the young people with whom I met felt they were accepted and listened to; felt they were being heard within the boundaries of Valleys Kids. They were not so sure about the world outside.

The next chapter shows that there are still many blocks in the wider population that need to be overcome. They prevent children and teenagers from being heard properly, even now. The following pages further address Valleys Kids efforts in shifting some of those barriers.

PART THREE

The Art of Listening

CHAPTER 7

Can You Hear Me - Now?

'The Welsh Government is highly focussed on giving a voice to children. Since Wales signed the UN declaration of Children's Rights, a few years ago, the government has been developing policies to ensure that children's rights are a reality and that all aspects of government pay attention to what they say. Furthermore, policy in Wales is moving from taking account of children's rights and welfare, toward putting a focus on their well-being.'

Education for All for the Well-being of Children – Wales 2007.

As we have learned from previous chapters, Valleys Kids has been listening to children and young people for a very long time. This organisation was developed with the forethought that young people should be *'given a voice.'* It has the unique experience of responding creatively to this issue and the main reason for writing 'Can You Hear Me?' is to share that gained knowledge, more widely.

At this stage, it seems essential to step back briefly from the creative energy of the Valleys Kids initiative and catch our breaths. Before we move on to more developments in this adventurous project, it is important to survey the changing attitudes towards working with young people in British society, generally. New challenges arise in listening to young people and their families. As well as observing

Valleys Kids from the angle of the local community, it also needs to be viewed from the perspective of what is happening nationally.

GROWING UP IN THE 21ST CENTURY

Attitudes towards working with young people and families have changed dramatically in the last 30 years: particularly since the onset of the new millennium. New legislation and policies present fresh challenges for organisations like Valleys Kids: in fact, anyone who has contact with young people. Quite rightly, protection of children is high on the agenda of most politicians but as will be argued later in this chapter – this too can have a limiting effect on the development of the young, if over applied.

Without doubt, we have made great progress in some areas of children's welfare since young people were sent to work down the pits, among the other huge demands that were put upon them. In the 19th century, children were needed and expected to help the family survive in a way that they are not required to do in this present time. Today, the prolonged childhood we enjoy in Britain was, until relatively recently, a luxury that few could afford. The role of being a child in the family has changed. It would seem we have come a long way since Victorian society placed great value on the phrase *'Children should be seen and not heard!'*

Politically, it has been a long, slow process to bring the rights of children as far as they have come. In the 1960s and 70s, the State assumed the right and began gradually to involve itself in the family. As a result, since the enactment of the Children's Act in 1989, young people in Britain have had by law a right to be heard and subsequent acts have further enforced and widened this legislation. So, in theory, it seems that society has moved quite a distance from excluding young people in having a say in their own destiny. However, in this present age, I would suggest many obstacles block this process of empowerment and it appears that adult society still struggles to make a reality of this plan of listening to our offspring. One aim of this chapter is to explore why it is so difficult and how we can overcome the ambivalence that surrounds the intention to give voice to our children.

Oppression of children is often considered a historical issue or something that occurs abroad, possibly in the third world. So when modern British society becomes aware of the extremes of today like sexual or physical abuse, it is shocked that young people can still be treated in this way in their home territory. The short lives and highly reported violent deaths of little children such as Victoria Climbie (February 2000) have helped galvanise into being the much-needed legalisation, which has created changes in attitudes and the ways we protect the young. In recent years, these cruel events have pushed our politicians to face the extreme violation of some youngsters and to start to deal more effectively with it. Continuing reports of similar deaths of young people show us that there is still more progress to be made in protecting our children who are at risk.

On the other hand, it is important to acknowledge that we are also neglecting to face the broader picture. In describing Valleys Kids, the purpose of this book is not only to dwell on the children at risk from violence and neglect. The plan is to include and support them in partnership with others while using a wider lens. The danger is that while we are focussing only on the extreme, we minimise and turn a deaf ear to what is happening with the majority of our

How skilled are we at encouraging all young people to become unique, creative and inspirational beings? To realize their potential?

children. Many of those are seeking ways of surviving (and are even blossoming) despite their historical legacy. Valleys Kids' continued role is to listen closely to the needs of the young and the families in which they grow up.

Certainly, as illustrated by the quotation on the previous page from the Welsh Government, politicians encourage us to engage with young people when considering their environment, their future, and their lives. The intention to listen to our youngsters appears to be alive in Wales, as well as the rest of the United Kingdom. Research projects have been set up, such as the Wales–wide Funky Dragon and closer to home, Fframwaith explored the needs of young people in Rhondda Cynon Taff. Valleys Kids is also in the process of developing its own internal evaluation survey. However, for some involved in working with young people and their families – nagging questions arise:

- How good is present-day adult society at actually hearing what they say?
- How adept are adults at understanding their requirements?
- In our fast 21st century lives, are we really paying attention to helping them express who they are, what they want?
- How skilled are we at encouraging all young people to become unique, creative and inspirational beings? To realize their potential?
- How well are we preparing them to be active responsible citizens of tomorrow?
- Once we know their opinions, how often are we able to follow through and give them what they ask for?
- At this time, have we adults collectively found the right mind-set, which is necessary to encourage the empowerment of our children?

Today, over 35 years after the closure of the pits, poverty continues to put the greatest constraints on our young.

Of course, there are parents who are absolutely dedicated to giving freedom of speech to their offspring but there are others who find it very difficult. If we, as the Welsh Government suggests, are *'putting a focus'* on the well-being of young people and we want more for them, do we not need to consider the questions above? If we are to pay more than lip service to including children in the democratic process, do we not need to review the sincerity of our intentions and even have the patience to evaluate our skills in listening to what they say? Perhaps we even need to take time to consider how we may unintentionally sabotage a plan, which is rooted in wanting the best for our children's welfare and well-being.

BLOCKS TO HEARING WHAT YOUNG PEOPLE HAVE TO SAY

This chapter intends to draw attention to some damaging trends that weaken modern society's resolve to listen to young people. We struggle with 'paying attention to what they say.' We say we want to hear them, we go to great lengths to research their needs and involve them in doing that: yet, in reality we fail to acknowledge the powerfully conflicting attitudes that destabilize this policy. Sadly, there are several, which include the following:

LIVING IN POVERTY

One of the main continuing silencers of children comes from living in poverty. Today, over 35 years after the closure of the pits, poverty continues to put the greatest constraints on our young.

While I am writing this in 2011, the news is just 'breaking' that the difference between the rich and poor in this country is now greater than it has been for 40 years. It is important to remember that 2010 was the Labour government's target year for halving child poverty. The intention is that it is ended it by 2020. Donald Hirsch author of Through Thick and Thin: Tackling Child Poverty in Hard Times (written for End Child Poverty in 2009) confirms that the present recession and rising joblessness has created a new crisis of poverty in Britain. Obviously, the conclusion is that having taken a few steps forward in lifting some of our children out of that oppressive atmosphere, they are now being sucked back into it.

It is easy to be complacent about poverty in our country. We can look towards Africa, South America or India through travel experiences or through the eyes of the media and see the extremes. We can congratulate ourselves for living in a country where life is not quite so difficult. The greatest majority of our children live in homes with a roof over their heads and running water. We can choose to deny the extent of the deprivation in Wales, that it has the highest proportion of children living in poverty in the whole of the UK. Part of the confusion is that there is no single, universally accepted definition of poverty. A Save the Children report states that an official definition of poverty in this country is that of a household making less than 60% of the national average. The European Union's working definition of poverty is: *'Persons, families and groups of people whose resources (material, cultural and social) are so limited as to exclude them from the minimum acceptable way of life in the member state to which they belong.'*

My past experience as a counsellor working with families devastated by addiction has shown me that where families are stressed, despite best intentions some parents have little time or energy to listen. Those who are poor often feel negative, inferior, passive, hopeless and powerless. As a result of living with great tension, they themselves cease or are unable to communicate and the children are often denied the effort it takes to help them to develop that skill of expressing who they are. The depression becomes cyclical: in turn, the younger generation learn to feel negative, inferior, passive, hopeless and powerless. Their health, their schoolwork suffer and the rift expands between the advantaged and disadvantaged; between the articulate and those who are less likely to find their voice; between those who are expected to do well at school and those who are not.

In recent years, the widening of the gap between rich and poor has been highlighted by our addiction to technology. According to Kirsty Young's recent BBC2 programme The British Family; *'Johnny Average has £1700 worth of equipment and toys in his bedroom.'* So, the feeling of exclusion intensifies for families who are not able to afford computers and the different gadgets demanded by this 21st century. Again, schoolwork suffers because so much of our education and homework is dependent on modern technology. In England, great effort has been made by the government to combat this problem by supplying computers with Internet access to low income families. In most areas, poor children in Wales have not had that support, as yet. Valleys Kids has homework clubs in some of its centres where young people have access to computers.

There is a saying, which quips that it takes 2 people to make a baby but a whole community to grow it. Even in Rhondda Cynon Taf, which has a good reputation for its warm community spirit, some families are denied that kind of support. A culture of blame pervades some of our neighbourhoods. Some struggling families have a tough time and have a judgemental finger pointed at them frequently - particularly if their child has deviated from the norm. Children who are living in the poverty trap need and deserve a great deal of attention and support (emotional as well as financial) – urgently. This has to be given with a great deal of sensitivity. They desperately need to be heard but to expose them even more as different or needy would do as much damage as ignoring the problem. Valleys Kids inclusive approach comes from the broader perspective of wanting the best opportunities for all our young people - of helping them to help themselves.

As highlighted in Chapter one, by Valleys Kids report Hidden Potential, helping families recover financially is only part of the answer. In our well-intentioned purpose of *'giving a voice to children'* it is very important that we appreciate how deeply generations have been silenced over the years and how much reparation needs to be done. Valleys Kids' hard work and experience highlight that it is not something that will be healed quickly. To be able to express ones-self, to have the courage to talk freely requires a great deal of trust. In this situation, trusting those who would like to help is something that needs to be earned. If we want to help children living in poverty find their voice, we have to form relationships, we have to be prepared to work long and hard at doing so. There is no quick fix.

LOW EXPECTATIONS

One of the most restricting issues of living in an area which is imbued with poverty is that nobody expects very much of you. Neighbourhoods, families, individuals all gain a reputation of behaving in a certain way, of being

'Like I was brought up in a school where I had teachers telling me (particular teachers) you're never going to become anything because you are from the Rhondda and like you are brought up with that all the time and I think we have got to get out of that mind frame.'

under-achievers. Sadly a number respond to wearing that cap because they believe that it fits. If you are told often enough that you have little chance of making a success of your life then you believe it. You give up without even trying.

Miranda Ballin, Coordinator of the ArtWorks team at Valleys Kids described this feeling of categorisation and shaping by the environment in her thesis when she quoted Sarah, one of the participants in her project: *'Like I was brought up in a school where I had teachers telling me (particular teachers) you're never going to become anything because you are from the Rhondda and like you are brought up with that all the time and I think we have got to get out of that mind frame.'*

Valleys Kids responds to this by aiming high. It provides opportunities to try different experiences, to meet different people, to expand the possibilities. It has provided tuition for people who are having difficulty at school. It has created chances for some of its young people who have rarely moved out of the local area, to travel abroad. It converted the community centre in Penygraig into a state-of-the-art building because it believes that the people of the valleys deserve as nice buildings as the people of Cardiff.

So much talent, so much creative energy is lost because of the growing gap between the poor and the better off. So much potential is submerged because someone is born into an area that has had a difficult history.

However, it is important to acknowledge that it is not just poor children who have difficulty in having their voice heard. To varying degrees, the greater majority are silenced in some of the following ways.

A CULTURE OF FEAR

Unconsciously, when we give into our fears, we undermine many of our best plans. Tim Gill, a writer on childhood and play, compiled a book actually called No Fear. In it, he discusses a pattern of growing adult intervention and over-protection, which minimizes risk at the expense of childhood experience. He describes this feeling as *'a generalised and insidious anxiety about safety that has found expression in fears for children even though they are statistically safer than at any point in human history.'*

He argues that traditional children's activities and experiences, which those of us from previous generations enjoyed, have been relabelled as troubling or dangerous. In some primary schools in the United Kingdom, games like tag which include running in the playground have been banned because the staff were concerned they were becoming too rough. The simplest of pleasures get throttled in our safety conscious culture. Health and Safety policies keep us ever vigilant lest young people come to physical harm. Lesley, one of the original members of the Bike Club mentioned in Chapter 2 is now a school dinner lady. She expressed her sadness about being *'not allowed to give children a cwtch'* if they trip, fall and hurt themselves. So fearful have we become of litigation, rules have been made which prevent us from cuddling a hurting child. When not at school, more and more children are kept at home under adult supervision and not encouraged to go out to play with friends, as did those of us who grew up in earlier parts of the 20th Century.

Of course, the safety and protection of children must be paramount. However, if we really want kids to communicate who they are, what they want – then we have to find ways of redressing the balance; giving them freedom to be, allowing them the stimulation and challenges of new experience, while providing safe boundaries. My dictionary gives one definition of experience as *'wisdom derived from the changes and trials of life.'* I wonder what lengths we are going to - to ensure that future generations develop that kind of good judgement? Surely, if we are moving toward putting a focus on our young people's well-being then the development of this kind of wisdom is absolutely essential? Yet, paradoxically, it appears that in our efforts to keep our children safe we are damaging and endangering their lives in another way. If we cannot support them in taking some risks then we may be crushing the development of their skills in learning to trust their own instincts. Most children have a sense of self-protection but it is imperative for their sake that we help them listen to and appreciate that wise inner voice of caution. The danger of being over zealous in our protection is that we stop them from hearing what their own common sense is telling them. We hinder them from discovering childhood as an adventure where independence is discovered. We hamper them from learning and forming their own decisions concerning their safety.

The most delightful aspect of children at play is to observe what shines through: the spirit of the child that survives, copes, experiments, creates and reinvents - and the joy that accompanies that self-discovery. In their angst, many adults have forgotten to honour and encourage that positive energy. In their over-protectiveness, they reign in that zest for life – too tightly. Professor Hugh Cunningham ends his book The Invention of Childhood (which is a study of childhood through the ages) with the sentence: *'To think of children as potential victims in need of protection is a very modern outlook, and it probably does no-one a service.*

Free play is a means in which children have the choice to work out and direct their own activities. With little adult interference, they are more likely to learn to negotiate with other kids; they may discover ways of communicating and they may find ways when they decide to argue their case - or not. When they have enough room to run around and to make as much noise as possible they can get rid of frustration, anger and other energies. Also, it gives them much scope to develop the imagination. Debra, who has been play coordinator at Valleys Kids for many years says, *'provide the material, give them the space to get on with it and it is amazing what they can create with a parachute or the branch of a tree.'*

In Valleys Kids playschemes adults are helped too. Summer brings challenges to families, which are more exaggerated than at other times of year. Having kids at home for 24 hours a day continually for more than 6 weeks of the year is hard, particularly if you are a single parent. There is no outlet from the noise, the energy and the demands. Time away from school can also be expensive for families. Therefore, summer playschemes are a very important part of the Valleys Kids programme – for children and for parents. When children come to play scheme, the pressure on the family is relieved.

THE AGE OF TECHNOLOGY

Perhaps one prime area of modern life where the better-off young people can be adventurous, curious and experimental while enjoying great freedom, results from the growth and spread of technology. No other age has experienced the ability to reach other cultures at the touch of a button, perhaps by experiencing Australian society while watching Neighbours, for example. These days, social contacts are not just developed in the street or in the school playground but from much further afield. The global world has become a much smaller place thanks to technology like mobile phones and the Internet. As young people learn to live more and more of their lives online, the very nature of childhood is being changed. Many have experienced it as a successfully interesting way to learn and pursue their interests. Social relationships are created online from the security and comfort of their bedrooms. According to the BBC News Website reporting on an Ofcom report (April 2008), 60% of children use social networking sites to make new friends compared to 17% of adults. As yet, many parents don't have the same technological agility as their offspring. In sharp contrast to other areas in life, the balance has swung the other way and many adults have put aside their concerns about privacy and safety on the net, believing wrongly they have been taken care of by someone else.

In the context of this book, while acknowledging some of the great benefits that modern technology brings, it is also important to examine some of the negative effects that television, computers, mobile phones, have on the skills of human communication. One of our concerns is that some children using the methods mentioned above are becoming isolated in their rooms and substituting virtual relationships for the day-to-day interaction which human relationships require. The need for youth clubs, for community organisations like Valleys Kids, which provide informal social situations where youngsters can participate in group activities while bonding, forming and maintaining friendships, has never been greater.

Sue Palmer who wrote Toxic Childhood argues that the electronic age 'can dumb our young people down.' She says that 'the more technology has allowed us to talk to *each other, the less we seem to talk to our children.*' The effects of television on very young children are alarming a number of people particularly when busy parents tend to use it as an electronic babysitter to keep their little ones amused. The BBC children's programmes are world renowned for the high quality of their children's programmes. They are planned well, often featuring a clear single voice that stimulates children into making a response. However, organisations like Talk to Your Baby, run by the National Literacy Trust, are now trying to raise awareness of the importance of switching off the TV, computer or mobile phone and concentrating at least some of the day on talking to babies. Research is showing us that very young children need human contact and communication to be able to develop their speech. The constant hum of technology and background traffic hampers that process: it may interfere with how much parents speak to their child. Television personalities reaching out through the media do not connect with or inspire very young people in the way that a close parental relationship does. Liz Attenborough, director of Talk to Your Baby, points out that we need to be aware of this but not to over react. She cautions us from '*throwing the baby out with the bath water!*' Some exposure to children's programmes provides a positive learning experience. This too is a matter of redressing the balance, of being free of all technological gadgets at some time in the day: of allocating space to give children more personal time and attention.

Some parents struggle to know how to communicate with their children, to know what to say. One of the aims of the Baby Club and Parent and Toddler groups at Valleys Kids is to support Mums and Dads in learning how to do just that.

THE LOSS OF THE FAMILY MEALTIME

One of my clearest memories of when I first joined the team of Valleys Kids was provided by a young man of about 13 years. I had discovered that a fruitful method of making contact with some young people was to set up a cookery station in the middle of a hall and prepare chicken curry. Some really interesting conversations arose from that but the most fascinating point for me was when we formalised things and sat down as a group to eat the meal. This young man thoroughly enjoyed his meal. He asked for more, but ate it all very quickly – standing up. When invited to sit down and join the rest of us he refused: he was very embarrassed. He said he never sat down to eat and obviously found conversation with his peers in this environment as very disturbing and uncomfortable. It could be argued that he was only one person in a group of about 30. However in discussing this with my colleagues who are practising as youth workers, he is not an isolated case. There are many youngsters who grow up in families where the norm is that each person finds an individual, ready meal in the fridge, warms it up in the microwave and eats it often unaccompanied, usually in front of the television.

American studies (University of Minnesota 2009) confirm that adolescents who participate in regular family meals have healthier diets and meal patterns, compared to those who miss out on these eating regimes. While strongly supporting the need for returning to, or finding new systems where children can learn to eat in healthier ways, it is also very important to argue for the need to recreate traditions where we make space and time for the family to communicate. While the emphasis has been on material survival, families have become busier as they struggle to make ends meet. As this process has been evolving, one of the sacrifices has been the family mealtime. In previous

One of the aims of the residential work is that young people can experience the making and sharing of a meal together, discovering mealtime as social occasion.

generations, as with some people today, this was a precious time of socialising, of catching up with gossip, passing on news, sometimes having a laugh, of consulting each other and making family decisions together. At best, it was often a space in the day allocated to listening to what both adults and children had to say. In contrast, it could also be a time of fear of learning to deal with conflict and uncomfortable feelings if one parent dominated the conversation. Mostly, there was some recognition that human beings of all ages yearn to be heard. In its most basic form, it was a training ground in communicating and forming relationships.

Perhaps families are finding a way of readjusting to this trend. Kirsty Young reported that parents of today do spend much more time with their children than they did in the 1970s: the emphasis being on quality time. However, our experience suggests that some families have lost this intergenerational anchor of taking time to understand and appreciate each other. As a result, that loss diminishes our capability of comprehending what the other is saying.

Valleys Kids has always taken groups of children on residential breaks away from the the their home area. It now owns a remote house on the Gower for that reason. It is called Little Bryn Gwyn. One of the aims of the residential work is that young people can experience the making and sharing of a meal together, discovering mealtime as social occasion.

CONFLICTING MESSAGES

When we do communicate with youngsters we can be very ambivalent in our approach. Children and young people receive such a negative press. Adult society is very clear in how we tell them what we do not like about them or what our fears are for them. It is rammed home over and over again in the form of statistics and news bulletins. We constantly hear on radio or on the television about children who 'terrorise their neighbourhoods ' who bully other children, who are drinking alcohol ever younger, who are obese and becoming couch potatoes, who become pregnant at an early age, who use make-up at too young an age, who self-harm and are developing more and more mental health problems. Although on the one hand, we romanticise childhood ('*the best years of your life'*), we also appear to be afraid of it and we are in danger of demonizing our young. Reports of children being violent with each other have probably contributed to this anxiety.

After the murder of 2 year old Jamie Bulgar by two ten year olds, a newspaper commented: '*We will never be able to look at our children in the same way again… parents everywhere are asking themselves and their friends if the Mark of the Beast might not also be imprinted on their offspring.*'(Sunday Times, 28th November 1993). It became an iconic case and raised huge political issues. The extent of the media coverage of the Jamie Bulgar case was unprecedented. The language used by the press was fearful and dramatic. Adult anxiety that was already high rose rapidly in response to the hype. Although extreme cases such as this are a rarity, children in general were no longer seen as quite as innocent. Since this time there appears to have been an increase in a suspicious, negative attitude towards children and childhood, generally.

To redress the balance we need to question how often we celebrate the positive, the creative, the energetic, and the inquisitive nature of childhood? As is illustrated all through this book, Valleys Kids does this well and often but I would hazard an educated guess that in society generally, the disapproval aimed at our young people greatly outweighs

*'I work so hard.
I do drama. I do
volunteer work. I
want them to see that
I am a creative and
responsible person.
Why can't they see it?'*

favourable opinions. Newspapers do not appear to be full of items focussing on the capabilities of children, on their successes: or on their ability to survive and blossom despite the challenges and problems of growing up in our present complicated age created largely by generations of adults.

During the interviews I met with one young woman who was about 19 years of age. She was feeling very indignant. Accidentally, she had been pushed into an older woman in a busy street. She suffered *'a load of abuse'* for bumping into her. The woman complained very loudly and very publicly about the youth of today. The girl who was relaying the story said, *'I work so hard. I do drama. I do volunteer work. I want them to see that I am a creative and responsible person. Why can't they see it?'*

It is important to say here that young people are not completely blameless. When talking to some of the original members of the Basement Project in Penygraig, several voiced a present day anxiety about a small proportion of youths hanging around on street corners and in alleyways. The adults, while appreciating the large number of youngsters who were attending the project, were concerned about and sometimes intimidated by groups of others who were not engaged in the activities. Fear of gangs of youths has added to the prejudice towards the young. However, a report commissioned by Communities First, researched by the University of Glamorgan (Professor Dave Adamson et al) suggests that there is a need for better communication with this particular group. The report comments: *'If someone believes they are not being listened to, then they generally are inclined to withdraw and disengage.'*

It is well documented that the early stages of the 21st century is a very confusing time for children growing into adulthood. (Work with Young People edited by Jason Wood and Jean Hine. 2009). In that book, Howard Williamson, Professor of European Youth Policy at the University of Glamorgan argues that modern youth policy in Europe including Wales, is *'imbued with paradox and contradiction.'* He goes on to state that mixed messages are given out about young people. *'On the one hand they are seen as participative and responsible citizens, on the other as potentially dangerous or risky individuals.'* We invite them to be highly involved in research about their well-being and futures while shouting loudly about the behaviours mentioned above. Different voices expressing conflicting points of view. One message says, 'we trust you', the other says 'we do not.'

Young people are usually very perceptive. They observe adult behaviour. They learn from it. Often, the reaction to contradictory messages is to be confused and not to trust: to feel alienated and not heard, to pull more closely together, to push up a protective barrier and to be careful with whom they communicate. We help shut them up. We discourage them from speaking their minds.

UNEASE ABOUT TEENAGE SEXUALITY

I visited all four of the areas served by Valleys Kids and asked each of the groups of young people a question – *'What is important about coming to the centre?'* In each of the areas the response was immediate. Among individual replies there were several common answers. *'It keeps me off the streets'* or *'it is somewhere to meet new friends* or *'I feel safe here, not judged.'* Interestingly, in every area (usually towards the end of the interview) some one said, *'Speaking to Jayne.'* Jayne Blacker is a nurse employed by Valleys Kids primarily to help young people deal with relationship and sexual issues.

When I asked why talking to Jayne was so important. I was told by one 16 year old that *'I can talk to her about anything. Without her help, I would never have gone to the family planning clinic or the doctor and I don't want to get pregnant like a lot of my friends. I wouldn't talk to my mam either.'* In each of the areas there was great appreciation for the fact that a specialist nurse was meeting them on their territory and building respectful, confidential relationships with the young people attending the clubs. She was seen as not judgemental, *'not heavy'* in her approach. *'She plays cards and has a laugh with us.'* One young man of 18 years said that if it hadn't been for these informal conversations, *'I would never really have thought about contraception.'*

One of the greatest blocks in communication between adult society and young people is in the preparation towards moving into adulthood. This is particularly relevant when addressing approaches towards sex and relationships. Valleys Kids believes that we should listen to teenagers when they say they want easier access to contraception. At this time, we make it quite difficult. For example:

- Schools may be encouraged to educate young people about relationships and sexuality but they are not allowed to supply condoms.
- Family planning clinics are not always accessible being a bus journey away. If you have no money or if bus timetables stop around 5pm and the evening clinics are from 5pm until 7pm then you are not being encouraged to attend.
- In these close-knit communities, fourteen and fifteen year olds do not want to walk in to a family planning clinic and find their mother's best friend sitting there.

If young people feel judged or disapproved of in clinics or surgeries as they often feel they are, they won't return for help. The contact and opportunity to reach out and help is lost.

Data from the National Office of Statistics (published in the Guardian in February 2011) show that there has been a small improvement in the number of teenage pregnancies between 2001 and 2009. However, the 2009 statistics for Rhondda Cynon Taff show that for every 1000 women from 15 to 17 years, 46.6 conceived. This is the second highest rate in Wales, behind Merthyr Tydfil where 60.7 out of 1000 fell pregnant. Although the national rates are the lowest recorded since 1985, the reality falls far short of the last British Governments pledge to half teenage pregnancies.

It would be easy to shake our heads disapprovingly and mutter about the irresponsibility of teenagers and their inability to say 'no.' However, if this situation is to improve, then surely we adults must look honestly at our own cultural beliefs and stances and compare how well we are doing in comparison with some of our European neighbours? How well do we prepare our future generations for loving, respectful relationships?

In 2006, Channel 4 produced a programme called Lets Talk Sex. It showed that the Netherlands have the lowest number of teenage pregnancies in Europe. In the UK our *'shameful statistics'* are 5 times higher. In Britain, we have the highest teenage pregnancy rate in Western Europe. The documentary went on to explain that Dutch sex education is effective because they focus on helping young people make responsible decisions about relationships and sex with the emphasis on mutual respect. From primary school age, children learn about biological detail AND also spend lots of class time discussing values and attitudes. Holland provides age-appropriate sex and relationship education from the time children start school.

Compare this with an Estyn report written in 2007 highlighting the patchiness of the effectiveness of primary schools in approaching this crucial topic. (The purpose of Estyn is to inspect the quality and standards in education and training in Wales.) This report states *'....either due to the censorious attitudes of governors and headteachers or, in some cases parents, in about a quarter of schools, teaching is solely limited to the topic of physical changes that take place at puberty, through a desire on the part of this group to protect children and delay them developing into young adults.'* It draws some of its data from a book entitled Freedom's Orphans: Raising Youth Awareness in a Changing World. This was produced by the Institute of Public Policy and Research. It claims that British teenagers are the most sexually active in Europe and purports that 25% lose their virginity before the age of 16. Peer pressure is viewed as a large contributory factor in this state of affairs. Also, it states that almost 1 in 3 of the 15 year olds who were questioned did not use a condom during their last sexual intercourse.

A confusing array of options and pressures along with a lack of informed knowledge moulds teenagers' frames of mind about sex and relationships. We do not make it easy for young people to cope with their powerful sexual feelings at a time when young women are at their most fertile. Great turmoil is caused by not being given the relevant information that would help them safely navigate their way to make considered choices. In fact, in our disapproval or reluctance to face the enormity of this challenge, we are placing them in danger not only of teenage pregnancy but also of learning about relationships from just as uninformed peers or from pornographic websites that really do not encourage mutual respect. We are turning a blind eye to the contraction of sexually transmitted infections, too. It is no fluke that Chlamydia has hit a new high in Wales. According to Dr Richard Lewis, (Welsh secretary of BMI) infection rates are highest in the age group of 15 to 24 years. Other STIs like the HPV virus which causes mouth and throat cancer in young men are on the rise too.

Again, the necessary requirement in reducing the number of teenage pregnancies and related health issues comes from building trusting and respectful associations. Part of Jayne's role is to provide condom clinics for those young people who require them. (Her professional approach is steered by the Fraser Guidelines ruled in the House of Lords in 1985). Among other intentions, this responsibility gives her access to young people who are difficult for other professionals to reach. She has spent 3 years establishing safe and confidential contact with young people who attend Valleys Kids centres. Some teenagers have been easier to help than others. Only now are some of the most wary beginning to spend 10 minutes with her talking through some of their concerns about relationships and sex.

A challenge that continues to be addressed is the connection between teenage alcohol abuse and early pregnancies. Forty per cent of teenage pregnancies are attributed to alcohol abuse. Young people may hear important information about contraception when they are sober. When they have been drinking heavily, the ability to choose wisely disappears.

The young men and women I spoke to want help with this very sensitive issue of sex and relationships. However, they

'Oh no! Someone else is going to talk about us as living in disadvantaged communities. How do you think that makes me bloody feel?'

are suspicious of where the help is coming from. They do not want to be judged: they want to be heard. Perhaps we adults need to accept that we are part of this serious cultural problem and reassess how we respond to the need for that support.

LABELLING

As I have been writing these pages, I have been very conscious of the fact that I have been using certain words to describe the social conditions in the South Wales valleys and not everybody likes that jargon. Words like 'deprived,' or 'deep and complex problems' or 'living in poverty.' In using them, I have been painting a picture of the dark side of the valleys. In one group that I visited one woman was extremely annoyed when I mentioned writing this book. She said, *'Oh no! Someone else is going to talk about us as living in disadvantaged communities. How do you think that makes me bloody feel?'* She has a very strong point. To be stuck with those labels is diminishing and negative. Adults as well as children can feel trapped under the weight of growing up with such descriptions and some cope by denying the reality of the conditions that still exist here.

However, Valleys Kids work is about moving forward, not staying caught in the problem. It demonstrates that there are choices: change is possible. Perhaps it is slow and at times more possible with the young. Confronting the labels and having support while using them as stepping-stones to make changes is positive and possible, if that is what individuals desire. Trying different activities and experiences, meeting new people in order to broaden horizons and see more clearly can help us feel more positive and in charge of our lives: building on the strengths of people in the community.

SO, CAN WE HEAR THEM - NOW?

The evidence given in this chapter would suggest that in responding to different crises, modern society has made SOME progress in listening to young people. The problem of excluding them from having a say in their lives has been acknowledged. Policies have been put in place to enable the process of improvement: to include them in decision-making procedures. However, the blocks mentioned in this chapter demonstrate that while the intention is good, the practice of listening falls far short of the mark, even now. One member of staff at Valleys Kids summed it up by saying, *'We have been given the policies but nobody in power has really created the strategies to tell us how to listen to children.'* We have to discover how as we move along. There is a general assumption that everybody knows how to do that: to listen well. Michael P. Nichols, who wrote a book, entitled The Lost Art of Listening, disputes that supposition. He says that *'Contemporary pressures have regrettably shrunk our attention spans and impoverished the quality of listening in our lives.'* Many adults have difficulty in hearing what others say, no matter what age.

As we know, the ethos of Valleys Kids comes from a community development approach, from a faith in the importance of each individual within the community. These core beliefs require attending to the young and their parents, of hearing what they have to say, of encouraging them to have a positive *'can do attitude'*; honouring who they are and encouraging them to explore the extent of their resourcefulness.

CHAPTER 8

Discovering A Voice

'I used to be really quiet and shy before. I am more talkative now, more confident since I started coming to Youth Theatre.'

'We used to get into a lot of trouble before we did drama. I use it to help me with anger management. It helps me be calm.'

'We are like a family. We trust each other. We come together and share how we feel.'

'ArtWorks has helped me a lot. I know what I can do now.'

The comments noted here come from excerpts of conversation with four young women attending the Rhydyfelin Youth Theatre, part of the Valleys Kids ArtWorks programme. Amy (aged 12), Carla (13), Rachel (13) and Emma (21) all talked animatedly about their experience in these groups and the ensuing impact on their lives. Together, they have given me the words that help in preparing the ground for this chapter that studies ArtWorks, the Youth Arts department of Valleys Kids. In particular, these next pages look at the influence ArtWorks has on the lives of some of the young people involved in its programme.

SETTING THE TONE

Throughout this book we have listened to the voices of the past telling us of the effects of history on the South Wales valleys; to the founders and staff of Valleys Kids who were inspired to provide a professional friendship, which in turn stimulated widespread networks of social support and attractive community buildings; to the people in the different communities who have endured great hardship and have had the courage and resilience to change their lot; above all to the children and young people who have inherited the ongoing effects of ruthless political decisions, but through Valleys Kids now have a legacy of community support which pushes for the finest opportunities of betterment.

We have considered some of the methods used to create that level of engagement, that essential tie of relationship. We have looked at the mediums of playwork, youthwork, volunteer work, community development work and different activities as ways of connecting with young people and their families, of opening up opportunities, helping them lift their expectations of life. During the research for this book 'Can You Hear Me?' young people have described how they feel rooted and safe within their particular Valleys Kids project, have been encouraged to spread their wings, to try new ventures, to raise their voices and to express who they are. In contrast, in the last chapter we have also considered some of the many ongoing societal blocks that continue to shut out and shut up our young, undermining their confidence and hindering their social development. In this chapter, to help redress the balance and find some ways of counteracting this oppression, we study another specialist method in helping young people find their voice. We look at the purposes of the ArtWorks team of Valleys Kids.

The following quote is taken from the thesis written by Miranda Ballin, ArtWorks co-ordinator who along with her team is responsible for developing this programme. The focus of her dissertation is the role of Youth Arts in Community Development. She draws on feedback from participants on some of the benefits of attending the drama groups. *'In contrast to their formal education experiences participants valued the social learning they experienced in ArtWorks. They particularly referred to the way they were able to receive positive criticism and develop their own critical thinking. They enjoyed learning and supporting each other in this process. There was evidence that the environment at ArtWorks encouraged them to trust and respect each other and helped develop their confidence.'*

According to Miranda, the method of the ArtWorks team comes from the practice of Youth Arts, mainly drama. In their work with young people, the team also embraces other art forms. Music, video-work, poetry, story-telling can also be included. Quoting further from her thesis, she describes Youth Arts as *'a generic term used to describe the practice of working through the arts with and for young people.'* In further discussion for the purpose of this book, she went on to elaborate that while the drama is important, a major focus of the ArtWorks team is the social development of young people. The whole concept is to help develop ideas, essentially encouraging youngsters to express what it is they want to say about many different issues related to their lives.

Historically, drama has been a part of Valleys Kids since the early days of the Penygraig Community Project. At first, large numbers of young people performed in different shows with ready prepared scripts. In 1990, under the auspices of Spectacle Theatre a youth theatre was established there for six months initially. After this,

Miranda (whose involvement with this project started then) continued to work independently on a project-by-project basis with no formal funding. In 1998, Valleys Kids was awarded 3 years lottery funding from the Arts Council of Wales to set up a Youth Arts project called ArtWorks. This allowed employment of 3 professionally trained Youth Arts workers to develop this method of working with the young in the 4 aforementioned community projects of Penygraig, Rhydyfelin, Penyrenglyn and more recently, Pen Dinas. The development of this work has continued to this day. In 2009 ArtWorks celebrated 10 years as a fully funded Youth Arts project and 18 years of youth arts practice. Different funding has enabled them to develop a larger team and spread their work further. Today the team consists of a highly experienced coordinator with social work qualifications; 3 youth artsworkers; another artsworker employed to work with those over 16; 2 graduate apprentices and a developmental and sustainability worker.

The practice of devised work, where young people developed the story line between them, started in the first Penygraig Youth theatre in 1990 after an experiment of trying to work unsuccessfully on a scripted piece provided by Spectacle Theatre. This teamwork method requires that the young people create the story, the ArtWorker writes the script with the approval of the group and together they produce and present a drama.

WHO IS HEARD HERE?

The business plan of ArtWorks (2010 – 2013) entitled Journey Makers, highlights 4 activity programmes coming under this specific umbrella with captions of Flight Paths, Growing Wings, Flightwings and Flying High.

The programme of Flight Paths covers drama workshops for the 7 to 13 year olds and Youth Theatre for 14 to 18 year olds. These are run on a weekly basis in all 4 Valleys Kids' key areas.

The business plan says of Growing Wings: *'We aim to reach young people where there are concerns that they are vulnerable and may potentially leave school with no education and training. We work alongside other agencies to encourage young people to attend our out of school provision in a supportive environment and to work within the schools to build confidence and develop new skills. We develop projects for young people who have little or no access to the arts. We work alongside other agencies to develop projects and programmes of work to meet the needs of the most vulnerable and isolated young people in our area.'* The ArtWorks team stated that because of the more informal atmosphere and the smallness of the groups, they are able to approach difficult behaviour differently from schools. They have discovered that they can work effectively with those in danger of being excluded from the educational system.

Flightwings is designed for those who are 16 plus. The drama work created in this programme is peer led. To graduate here from Youth Theatre or Growing Wings does not necessarily mean that a young person has to be the most talented actor. The place is earned more by commitment rather than ability. The ArtWorks team were very clear that their role was to lift higher those who need it most, to widen opportunities to those who are less likely to find them because of their personal circumstances.

Similarly to the other programmes mentioned in this chapter, the youth artsworkers offer mentoring and support. This may focus on personal problems or it may include helping with different kinds of school or college work. Gemma, who is responsible for developing the Flightwings programme, felt that the homework support was extremely important. Without it, there would be a considerable drop out rate from education. Within the ArtWorks remit, training and volunteer placements are made available to young people attending schools, colleges or university. Also, those who are unemployed are engaged with opportunities to develop confidence and self esteem, enabling them to make positive plans for the future.

Flying High encompasses international work. ArtWorks has developed links with many countries including Catalonia, Palestine, Jordan, Botswana, Malawi, South Africa, Italy and Brazil, with the purpose of enabling participants to attend international conferences and be involved in National as well as International arts exchanges. The opening up of dialogue with people from other cultures encourages young people to develop a sense of their place in a global context, expanding horizons far beyond the containment of the South Wales valleys.

As with other projects of Valleys Kids there are not really any rules within ArtWorks. Nevertheless, it is expected that those taking part will do the following:

- Work as a team
- Respect people and property
- Listen.

NURTURING THE VOICE

While the above paragraphs describe the wider picture of the ArtWorks team, great emphasis is placed on the social development of each child within the support-group setting

'Being listened to means that we are taken seriously, that our ideas and feelings are recognised and ultimately that what we have to say matters.'

of creative arts. Attention is given to nurturing the self-confidence of everyone who attends, encouraging them to form opinions, find their voices and express them. The educational method of ArtWorks comes from *'mucking in'*, from doing it from a position of being involved, from a belief that everybody is equal and important to the creative process. During discussion, all who participate sit in the inclusion of a circle – not in rows. In the practice of groupwork, there is some instructional coaching given by the pair of workers but the primary emphasis is on drawing out the creativity of the youngsters. Tom, one of the artsworkers summed up the encouragement given to each of the participants. He believes that the positive focus of this style of teaching conveys the message: *'The answers are within you.'*

Or, as Michael P. Nichols wrote in his book The Lost Art of Listening: *'Being listened to means that we are taken seriously, that our ideas and feelings are recognised and ultimately that what we have to say matters.'* Nurturing the voice or attending to what is within is fundamental to caring for the person and to helping draw out potential.

Some young people growing up in the South Wales valleys experience the reality of not being listened to, of not being taken seriously, of not having their feelings and ideas recognised, and as a result, of not believing that what they have to say matters. In several of the projects I encountered youngsters who have had to cope with prejudice from others because of the fact that they live in this area. One young man who lives in this area and who has socialised in Cardiff said he had been jeered at and informed that he must 'live in a cave'; others had been put down at school or in the workplace and told not to expect too much from their lives 'because they came from the Rhondda.' If you grow up in an area that has a reputation for being 'shit,' it is hard to believe that anybody wants to hear what you have to say. A further danger is that you become skilled at keeping your head down, at keeping quiet. Even worse, you shut down and learn not to have opinions.

The experience of being involved with the ArtWorks projects goes far to counteract this negative experience. I attended a drama workshop in Rhydyfelin where a small group of 7 to 13 year olds were working together with Rachel and Ian, the youth artsworkers, developing a storyline about a battle between elves and gnomes. Intertwined within this tale was another plot about a family deeply affected by receiving a letter from a father who had failed to return home from the Second World War. What I witnessed was a group of young people who were very focussed on what they were creating. They supported each other's ideas and seemed excited about formulating the plot together. At the same time, they were learning to place their creation in a historical perspective. For example, they considered whether Bob Marley's music was appropriate to play in the background. Although it was 'from the old times' he was not around in this period. Also, they wondered in the drama if it was an option during a time of rationing to send the kids out to buy chips.

As an exercise in understanding and portraying the feelings of the elves and gnomes in battle, the children were asked to express the body language of someone who was happy, angry, sad, and grumpy, among many other emotions. Indirectly, in tackling this task with great enthusiasm, these young people were learning to recognise the way these feelings looked and how they could be conveyed to others. They were able to label different emotions; they were learning to give importance to hearing how other people feel. In addition, throughout the process they appeared to really enjoy communicating with facial and bodily expressions.

It is important to acknowledge that some of the group come from families where they have to cope with such difficulties as surviving on a low income or being primary carer for a poorly mother. When there is stress within a family, members can shut down and repress how they feel in order to cope with the situation. Communication can deteriorate because different feelings are not recognised. Charles Whitfield who wrote a book entitled Healing the Child Within says: *'Troubled families tend to deny feelings, especially the painful feelings of the members. The child – and many of the adults – are not allowed to express feelings....'* If that is the case here, the children within the ArtWorks group are being given the opportunity to put this right by articulating emotions and learning about their significance.

As they enacted different scenes, the importance of being heard by staff and peers, of listening to each other shaped the essence of this well thought out exercise. The approach was gently encouraging. A little girl, who was new and shy, was not pushed beyond her abilities. She was praised for her first attempts. At the same time, an older member of the group was having her confidence boosted by being given some responsibility for encouraging and helping the younger members. She appeared to be enjoying that role. Peers and staff respectfully supported all ideas and suggestions towards developing the play.

The level of engagement and trust is of primary importance in helping children discover their voice. Reliable relationships between peers as well as between Artsworkers and young people are essential in this method of groupwork. Tegan, another member of the ArtWorks team explained, *'Knowing it is their support group is almost as important as knowing it is a drama group. In fact, the relationships are more important than the quality of work.*

**'If you don't have
close relationships,
you don't have the
quality of work.'**

*If you don't have close relationships, you don't have the
quality of work.'*

ENCOURAGING THE VOICE TO COME THROUGH

Some young people have difficulty expressing themselves
through the spoken word but with some help from
others discover that they can articulate their thoughts,
feelings and opinions quite clearly through the medium
of writing. Through this vehicle they may discover a way
of communicating, which in turn helps them to feel less
isolated and more included.

I spent a pleasurable Sunday morning taking part in a
creative writing group that had been given the name 'Hear
my Voice.' Maxine, another member of the ArtWorks team
whose background is in teaching English, had set this up 'to
help those whose voice is difficult to hear, whose words are
almost drowned out by other more confident members of
the ArtWorks groups.'

Kate O'Reilly, a writer from West Wales who works with
Disability Arts Cymru, facilitated this group. Along with the
rest of the gathering, I learned to describe fire through the
medium of Haiku (a Japanese form of poetry). I realised
very quickly that although I have been writing on a fairly
regular basis, I was the one who was stiff in my search for
descriptive language. My younger groupmates, (many of
whom started the session expressing great fear of writing)
were much more adroit and adventurous in painting
pictures with words. As in other ArtWorks groups, the work
done here was in fiction but many of the stories appeared
autobiographical, coming from their own personal
experience.

There were 8 young people between the ages of 12 and 17

attending this group. The majority had become inhibited in expressing themselves vocally, for different reasons. One girl was blind, several had struggled to manage dyslexia, some had failed English at GCSE level and had dismissed themselves as stupid and others were extremely shy. Some were there in the role of helper, as well as receiving help themselves. Each had been selected to attend the workshop to help raise their confidence and as a reward for their commitment to ArtWorks.

Kate was enthusiastic in her praise and she gave constructive criticism. In a later discussion, Maxine shared her opinion that the critique had been done in a positive and caring way, helping the kids know that their writer was trying to get the best out of them. Clearly, the facilitator was showing an interest. Being questioned by her encouraged them to believe that their work really mattered, really was good enough and that what they had to say was important.

Writing is often seen as a solitary task. However, this group was sociable, interactive and supportive. Sometimes, people wrote together. A few read aloud what their friends had written if they were too shy or had difficulty in doing so and others helped each other find an appropriate word. At the end of each exercise, different stories and poems were read out to all assembled. By lunchtime, when the workshop came to a conclusion, some of the quieter ones were volunteering feedback to their peers, in front of everyone present. Opinions, creative thoughts and feelings were all being expressed. Certainly, confidence had risen during the process of the morning.

The observation from other members of the ArtWorks team is that involvement in this creative writing project has brought about a positive response. Having support, while attending on an almost monthly basis has helped different individuals return to their original group and let their voice be heard more clearly.

FEELING ROOTED

The discussion on the importance of having a support group was continued when I visited 13 young people belonging to the Flightwings project while they were on a residential course in Little Bryn Gwyn (Valleys Kids' house on the Gower peninsula). This group consisted of members aged 16 to 25 who came from Rhydyfelin, Penygraig and Penyrenglyn. They were unanimous in their opinion of this need for ongoing support, as they had to deal with *'heavy stuff'* in the process of creating their plays. They appreciated the caring and feedback from their friends. This conversation arose after they produced for me the drama that they were creating around the topic of relationships. As I watched and listened I was slightly shocked that there was such an emphasis on the black side of relationships, on divorce, abuse, violence and rejection, to name a few topics. When I questioned this, I was given 3 answers:

1. Happy relationships are not so interesting as unhappy ones.
2. Some of the group experienced such painful situations at home and *'putting on a mask'* or *'being someone else'* helped them detach and work through the feelings involved. At the same time, those who were not experiencing abuse in their family felt they were able to understand more easily what their friends were going through and as a result believed that they could give more support.
3. When the drama was ready, it was going to be performed in 4 different venues – the Atrium at the University of Glamorgan, the Pop Factory in

Porth, Rhondda Women's Aid and Soar Community Centre in Penygraig. It was intended to help provoke constructive discussion on domestic violence with a wider audience.

The ever recurring theme that has woven its way through all the chapters in this book popped up again: the need to feel safe and the appreciation from young people that Valleys Kids fills that gap. I asked the members of Flightwings the same question that I had asked in every other part of the organisation: *'What does being involved in this group mean to you?'* Some of the answers came up in discussion. Others were written down for me. I list a sample of them:

'To me Flightwings is a place to be myself, not be judged.'

'Flightwings is a place for us to experiment and learn in a safe environment. It pushes us to succeed…'

'Flightwings is a place with no formalities. I feel more at home here.'

'I love coming here because it gets me away from the problems at home.'

'It takes you away from your own life and gives you a chance to be young and free.'

'I love the fact that you can be yourself but at the same time be someone else. When I am in drama I forget all the troubles I have in my life.'

'I feel respected here.'

I was touched by the openness of all these replies. I was deeply stirred by the response of one young woman (aged 16). She asked to talk to me because she didn't know how to write her answer to this question but wanted me to know and pass on what her involvement in Flightwings meant to her. Having come up through Youth Theatre, she was a fairly new member of this particular group but she knew she was accepted within this system and felt held within the group of friends. Her family has had to cope with an extremely painful and difficult time because her beloved elder brother committed suicide just over a year ago. I quote, *'The first place I thought of going to was Soar Centre. Miranda just sat with me and was quiet. It was what I needed. My family was chaotic. In Flightwings I can be myself again. I am the youngest sister again. It makes me feel safe.'* She went on to say, *'I have a young nephew, my brother's son who has a dramatic streak. I want to say to him, "Don't worry. When you are old enough I know a place where you can go, where you can feel safe".'*

I questioned her on whether she really wanted me to share these deep and very personal feelings. Very generously, she said she thought she did. She knew where to go, whom to approach when she needed help but what she is highlighting is the lack of formal support in the community for families who go through this very traumatic experience. I checked Rhondda Cynon Taf's strategy for reducing self-harm in children and young people in this area. They refer to the National Public Health Service for Wales. Although suicide is recognised as one of the highest causes of death among young people in Wales; although the number of deaths due to suicide is twice as high as those due to road accidents in this country; although those living in deprived areas of Wales are almost twice as likely to die from suicide as those from the least deprived areas (particularly young men) and although strategies are being put in place to try and lower this statistic, I can find no mention of care for the families who live on, coping with this terrible grief.

Providing an atmosphere of security for the members is high on the agenda of the team of artsworkers. The groups are kept small (maximum 20 people) generating a more intimate setting. Recognising the difficult situations that several of the young people are coping with and supporting them while they work through them are priorities in this project. Close communication with relevant colleagues in the broader team of Valleys Kids ensures that the safety net is spread even wider. Youth artsworkers link in partnership with youthworkers to ensure the strongest system of support for each participant.

Moving from Youth Theatre to Flightwings can mean shifting from one familiar support group to one less well known. So, the policy is that individuals can be members of both projects until they feel comfortable enough to commit and feel safe within the new group – when they feel they belong. In the wide spectrum of ages it is recognised that each individual is moving at a different pace and that they are all at different stages. Acknowledging and containing all those varied rhythms helps each person feel protected and rooted.

As we have discussed in other chapters, one of the greatest anxieties for young people growing up in the valleys comes from the lack of prospective employment. With this in mind, Gemma has developed links with Careers Wales and Flightwings is creating possibilities for future employment by providing opportunities for participants to gain different work skills. Over 20 young people have participated in workshops this summer, training as volunteers working with younger groups through the medium of drama. Others have learned about light rigging or have trained in other technical skills such as soundtrack work and filmmaking. With the purpose of increasing confidence, these abilities will look good on CVs and are geared to help open up

'It was somewhere to hangout, something to do, a distraction from all the crappy things that are easy to get into when you are a teenager.'

opportunities in future careers. The creative industries such as arts, television, filmmaking, and music all enjoy high profiles for providing employment in Wales.

SPREADING WINGS

'I know what I can do now.'

At the beginning of the chapter, these powerful words of self-assurance were spoken by Carla. There are other examples of young people gaining similar levels of confidence from being involved with ArtWorks and finding ways to express themselves. That self-knowledge marks the promise of huge potential.

One very good example of someone who found her promise, her courage to fly the nest and soar is Claire. In retrospect, from the position of being 25 years old, she describes her attraction to ArtWorks. *'It was somewhere to hangout, something to do, a distraction from all the crappy things that are easy to get into when you are a teenager. I had started to get into smoking a bit of pot, drinking on street corners. Drama was like a bright light, something to hang on to. ArtWorks took me outside the Rhondda, even though I was still in the Rhondda. We explored things that were going on in other parts of the country, other parts of the world. It broadened my mind. I became passionate about drama.'*

She also volunteered, *'At that time, it was like a war zone at home. Mam and Dad were fighting a lot. They thought that kids couldn't hear. I felt pushed out. Drama allows you to look at your own life. We did a piece on aggressive behaviour. When you stand back and see it objectively you can work out what you are feeling, what you want to say.*

Through drama I was able to say to them that this wasn't right.'

Gradually, through her involvement with ArtWorks and her other connections with Valleys Kids, Claire did find her way out of the Rhondda. It opened her eyes to new possibilities, spurred her on to reach for more in life. The ethos of the drama group made her want to achieve, ' *to get off my butt and make it happen.'* So she applied herself, she got the GCSEs that she needed and earned a place in university in Carmarthen. *'I loved university. I felt empowered. I thought, ' I've done this, I've got the grades'.'*

Since gaining her degree, Claire has continued to have many adventures. Among them, she has worked in Germany for a year, touring schools as an actor/facilitator so that kids could learn English in a fun and entertaining way; she has travelled to different parts of England as an actor in educational theatre, running workshops about different issues like bullying and racism; she has appeared in Panto in Wrexham and has worked as a playworker for Valleys Kids. Sometimes, she struggles to find the balance between the comfort of the familiarity of her home area, her family and friends in the South Wales valleys and knowing that *'things will only happen out there.'* She has decided that what she wants to do is to establish herself as a youth artsworker. She enjoys working with kids and likes using drama as a vehicle so that young people can view their world and have the opportunity to change their circumstances, if they want to. Claire wants to pass on the experience that she has had.

'It made me feel safe, included, that big arms were wrapped around me. When you feel you are being pushed out of one thing its nice when arms are opened on another side. It makes you feel accepted; that what we had to say

was worth it, listened to. People at Valleys Kids wanted to hear what we thought.'

THE LAST WORD

Continuing with the theme of the importance of listening to young people, the final comment in this chapter must go to members of Rhydyfelin Youth Theatre who were invited in 2010 to give a performance at the launch of the Strategic Plan for Rhondda Cynon Taf. Their specific brief was to create a piece of theatre that highlighted issues around child poverty.

Along with their youth artsworkers, the young people prepared the groundwork; they drew on their own sometimes intimate knowledge and experiences; they formed important questions; they found and projected their voices and produced their play in 4 different venues in Rhondda Cynon Taf and Cardiff, including St David's Hall.

They have found the skills and courage to articulate their thoughts and feelings. Carefully, we must consider how we reply to the questions they ask. Are we ready? Can we really hear what they are saying? Are we able to respond creatively or constructively? Do we have answers? Can we facilitate change enough so that we can meet their needs?

The youngsters called their creation Reality Bites. I quote directly from their description of the play. It is a piece created by young people who live in a Communities First area. It is their words, their story.

'Reality Bites is a short and powerful new play based on a day in the life of one young girl – Danni. We learn about her family, a family living near the edge of poverty, a family stretched to breaking point.

But humans are not elastic. Push them too far and they will break.

Reality Bites asks us some hard questions, such as why do some people live in poverty while others have plenty? And what can we do to change this situation when the world we live in seems to value people for what they own rather than who they are?

We know these are important questions to ask.'

CHAPTER 9

The Sounding Board of Family

*'With all the emotional baggage I carried with me, …
wondering how to pay the bills, remembering the next
court date to sort out contact with my kids' dad etc…
my two 'babies 'came into the firing line. Some days
it was as much as I could do to take them round the
corner to school. I didn't really want to go out the door,
but I had to. Sometimes, on days when I knew I should
be taking them to the park to play in the sunshine, I
selfishly elected that we stay at home. I was afraid that
they'd ask for ice-cream and stuff that I couldn't afford,
or want me to run around with them, which frankly, at
the time just felt like it would take too much effort. All
I wanted to do was sit. I had no energy, no motivation,
no 'oomph'.'*

Looking back at an earlier period of her family life, Vicky
wrote the account above describing her struggles. At that
time she was a single mother who was suffering from
depression. Many parents involved with Valleys Kids
describe similar difficulties in coping with their lives and
their families on a day-to-day basis, of feeling trapped in a
vicious cycle.

Vicky was a member of Valleys Kids' Feeling Good group in
Penyrenglyn. Her health visitor, who was concerned about

*'I have been able
with the help of the
group to move on, to
set my sights higher
and to get closer to
being the kind of
mum I aspired to be.'*

the isolating effects of depression on this mum and her
children, referred her there. Over time, Vicky responded
positively to the set-up of informal support in the group, as
well as to the healing from the complementary therapies
she received. Gradually, she went on to train as an
alternative therapist herself and now helps others who are
in a similar position to the way she was. She sums up her
sense of achievement, *'I have been able with the help of
the group to move on, to set my sights higher and to get
closer to being the kind of mum I aspired to be.'*

A TRADITION OF FAMILY SUPPORT

From the early days of the Penygraig Community Project,
Valleys Kids has always supported families. Although its
name would suggest that it works only with children, it
strives to include all age groups, from *'cradle to the grave.'*

Dave's story shows how families have a lasting involvement
with this voluntary organisation and how the relationship
is often about give and take. He was a long-term volunteer,
who among other tasks transformed part of the garage
space at the Penygraig Community Project into a gym,
clearing out the building and raising money for equipment.
He had become involved with the Bike Club through his
son Craig who has Downs Syndrome. Craig originally
became involved in the project when he was a baby. He
attended Eirlys and Ruth's first parent and toddler group
with his mum in 1979. Staying for a number of years, he
went on to take part in many activities including drumming
workshops and different performances on stage. Penygraig
Community Project helped him become involved with
Rhondda Community Arts by arranging transport to
rehearsals and performances. The arts have continued to be
a very important part of his life. His brother and sister (now
in their 30s) were youth clubbers in their time. Now, the
next generation attend the new centre in Penygraig.

Several of the families interviewed mentioned that down through the years different generations have become involved in a variety of activities in their particular community centre. The early records of Penygraig Community Projects show that as well as the informal support received by mums in the parent and toddler groups, women's groups were established, free and ongoing Community Access to Technology course was developed to help train different age groups in computer skills, aiding the possibility of employment. (As Valleys Kids grew, this project was extended to all of its centres, with the playbuses bringing the service into other communities. Over 1000 people have upgraded their IT skills as a result of this training.)

The centre in Penyrenglyn grew through contact with Health Visitors and the initial communication from Rhydyfelin came through Social Services, in conjunction with the research of the Bridges Community project. These community developments were set up, pushed by concerns about the health of mothers and children as well as worries about groups of disaffected youth. In Pen Dinas, Surestart also highlighted the need for support of families for children of all ages. As different methods of intervention grew, several of the parents became volunteers, helping the staff run these groups. Mums and dads were encouraged to take part in preschool playgroups, parent and toddler groups, after school play sessions and play schemes during Easter and Summer holidays, socialising and helping each other with different problems as well as being there for the kids.

In every centre, families felt encouraged to drop in, finding support for whatever problem they were coping with. Coordinators of the different projects and family workers have extended a professional friendship to people where there have been issues such as loneliness or isolation, concerns about discipline, fears of sexual or physical abuse, worries about coping with debt, health problems, alcohol and drugs related problems, relationship problems or educational problems. There are often enquiries about where to find appropriate assistance for different matters. Being in the centre of the community and having long established relationships makes it easier for adults as well as younger people to reach out for help in these venues. Frequently, the role of the organisation is to be a sounding board for local families. The members of the women's group in Rhydyfelin explained: *'You need someone you can turn to, someone you can trust.'* As I interviewed different parents, the phrase *'not judged'* was used frequently to describe their association with the Valleys Kids centre in their area. Generally, there was a wariness of being rated poorly because of low income, low educational achievement; of being perceived as *'not good enough.'*

The organisation's purpose is to support the adults in the family by listening, by making suggestions, by encouraging them to do things they would not have tried themselves and by referring on to an appropriate agency, where necessary. Solutions include running different kinds of support groups, building self-confidence through volunteer work or different kinds of training courses. Also Valleys Kids offers opportunities for families to take part in activities together or alternatively, by offering families time apart through individual activities and residential experiences away from home. As a result, through helping to widen the perspectives of the parents or grandparents, the children are given the chance to appreciate their own value, to improve their lot and to expand their lives even further.

In turn, being given the opportunity to open up the children's world raises the spirit of well-being in the family.

'If the children are fulfilled – it has a positive effect on family life.'

Eileen who works for Valleys Kids in Pen Dinas says: *'If the children are fulfilled – it has a positive effect on family life.'* The benefits are cyclical.

FRESH BEGINNINGS

Valleys Kids received a grant from the Big Lottery's Way of Life funding programme over a period of three years (2008- 2011) for a project named Fresh Beginnings. This was intended to promote healthy attitudes and lifestyles for children of 12 years and under, along with their families. As well as creating 'healthy slots' in the Valleys Kids' programme with taster courses on healthy eating and exercise, it opened up all sorts of opportunities and new challenges. Parents had the option of learning to cook healthily while on a tight budget. The project enabled people to go out of their home area for a while. Families experienced good old-fashioned day trips to the seaside and played games together on the beach – something quite novel for some of the younger generation from the valleys. Adults and children went camping together. A trip to Little Bryn Gwyn on a kite-making course gave at least one family a common hobby. Since then they have had great pleasure in flying kites together. Kids enjoyed exciting activities like horse riding and gorge walking.

Anne, who coordinated this project, believes that the donation of this band of funding has helped changed a lot of people's outlook. It helped some parents see that Valleys Kids was much more than a baby-sitting service for their children, and that it is there for the benefit of everyone in the home. Because of personal financial circumstances, venturing out to try different activities as a family has been a restricted option for many. If you don't have a car, it is difficult to travel anywhere. If you have a large family, public transport is expensive and therefore exclusive. Healthy living encompasses so much more than a good diet or regular exercise. It includes the uplifting of spirits. Fresh Beginnings was able create new experiences for adults as well as children. It provided the opportunity and time for having adventures, together.

As with the summer playschemes, for a period of time life changes and families have the opportunity to expand their horizons together. Consequentially, while taking part in some of the joint activities, parents learned that having fun together and keeping the young ones entertained does not have to be expensive. They discovered that new, stimulating and enjoyable times could be within reach for them, too.

The paragraphs above describe some of the universal services provided by the organisation to support the family network. As the following pages suggest, specialist help is also provided for specific family problems.

FEELING BETTER

A review from the Bridges Community Support scheme (October 2003- March 2004) mentions the Community Advocate, Andrew Hopkins. Among other responsibilities, he was *'involved in a number of cases including an employment tribunal, consumers rights, debt management, compensation claims, disability living allowance claims, benefit entitlements, legal advice on intestacy and wills, anti-social behaviour orders and neighbourhood disputes.'* Andrew was a lawyer employed by Valleys Kids to speak on behalf of different individuals seeking specific help in each of the communities.

'When I started to feel more relaxed and confident, it had a positive effect on the kids. I was able to lighten up, to have more fun, to become more tolerant. The reward was the smiles on their faces.'

He was also instrumental in setting up the first men's support groups in 3 of Valleys Kids' communities. These were a part of the Feeling Good programme and a follow up to the women's groups. The groups were devised to support adults who were isolated in the community or suffered from depression. Group and professional support was on hand to help with a variety of problems. Complementary therapists shared their skills of reflexology, reiki healing, head and body massage to help those that wanted it to relax and feel better about themselves.

One dad shared how his participation in the group combined with the advantages of the therapies set him up for the weekend by helping him relax, giving him the energy to cope with his son who suffered from aspergers syndrome and ADHD. Many reported that when the adults felt better their children benefited.

Vicky from the beginning of this chapter assesses her experience. *'It was nice to think that people thought I was worth investing their time and resources in, when I didn't and wasn't feeling myself. When I started to feel more relaxed and confident, it had a positive effect on the kids. I was able to lighten up, to have more fun, to become more tolerant. The reward was the smiles on their faces.'*

Kerstin Hamme-Hategekimana along with the University of Glamorgan completed a research into the effectiveness of the women's groups in 2006. Among her conclusions she states: *'The results of the year long research have shown that The Feeling Good groups respond to the needs of the women in the community, work effectively and empower women and families.'*

These groups still continue in Penyrenglyn and Rhydyfelin. The emphasis is on helping participants feel better

both physically and emotionally. As well as receiving group support and therapies, people are given different opportunities for volunteer work and training courses, helping raise further feelings of self-esteem. Some are helped towards a return to the work place; others reciprocate by contributing in many ways towards the uplifting of their community through their voluntary work.

FAMILIES STRUGGLING IN A DIFFICULT CLIMATE

If the primary remit of the organisation Valleys Kids is to work with children and young people, let us consider why they want to support and work with families? Traditional youth work tends to concentrate on the young in isolation from the wider community.

In recognising the tough conditions with which many families from the valleys communities have to deal, the aim is to help children through working in tandem with their parents, when needed. The organisation is well aware of and sensitive to the day-to-day stresses with which many parents live, particularly in earning enough to make ends meet. Valleys Kids strategic plan for 2006 to 2009 entitled Building on Success states that one of its aims is: *'Supporting families to explore the challenges that face them and help them work together to find solutions to those challenges.*

Before we go any further, it must be said that Rhondda Cynon Taf does not have the highest rate of child poverty in Wales. Indeed, according to the Bevan Foundation's report named 'What is Poverty? '(2010), it is fifth in the 22 areas which make up the country of Wales, coming behind Blaenau Gwent, Merthyr Tydfil, Cardiff and Newport. In this county, the number of children (between ages 3 and 15) whose families received Tax Credits while living in a household with an income of less than 60% of the median income for Wales was 13,315. (In the Principality, this is the line which decides whether someone is living in poverty or not.) Keep in mind that these figures were finalised in 2008 before the effects of the latest recession really kicked in and more people found themselves back in unemployment. Also, be aware that the take-up of tax credits is not universal so the figure may well underestimate the number of homes trying to survive below the threshold. Additionally, we must not forget that there are many children living in families hovering just above that defining poverty margin which is lower here in Wales than in other parts of the UK. To sum up, it is important to acknowledge that we are discussing a large number of children in this area who are living in families struggling to survive on very low incomes.

The report mentioned above goes on to state that *'There is a strong link between educational achievement and low household incomes, as measured by entitlement to free school meals.'* Children entitled to free school meals achieve at lower levels than children who are not entitled, at all Key Stages. This gap exists in English, Maths, and Welsh First Language. Also, there is a close relationship between free school meal entitlement and absence from school.

Further evidence from the Bevan Foundation suggests that less than a third of 18 to 24 year olds entering full time higher education were from lower socio-economic groups. In addition, the lower peoples' qualifications are, the more likely they are to lack (but want) paid work. A smaller proportion of people from less skilled socio-economic groups have participated in any 'learning activity' since leaving formal education.

Therefore, it can be assumed that morale, self-confidence and the motivation to succeed, are low in some poorer households. Parents who had a negative experience with education are less likely to encourage their children to engage with the school system. Candida Hunt writes in her manual The Parenting Puzzle, *'Adults' attitudes and ways of behaving influence a child's attitudes, behaviour and self-esteem.'* Unless checked, the devaluing pattern ripples down through the generations.

INHERITED ATTITUDES

Many families who struggle with low income (whether unemployed or working) have difficulty believing they have a right to reach for higher aspirations. These financial positions effect the perception and attitudes of individuals and families about where they come in *'the pecking order'* of our society. They assume that success is not meant for them. Most have problems envisaging that objective for themselves and several resist expecting a better life for their children, even if they want it.

The family network is the main system in which children learn to define and value themselves. Primarily, it is where they learn to formulate opinions and feelings; it is where they can become skilled at expressing who they are. In adolescence, most children use their primary relationships as a mirror or a sounding board to work out what they think, what they feel and what is right for them. Quite often, they kick against that board as part of the growing-up process.

When adults don't feel emotionally nurtured themselves, when they may be grappling with mental health issues, when they feel anxious about lack of money, of their

When a parent believes 'I am a valuable person', he or she is more likely to pass on that message of self-confidence to the young ones.

inability to feed kids properly or pay the heating bills to keep them warm, they can pass on their fears and negative ways of thinking to the younger members of the family. Anxiety makes it hard to listen, to tolerate the huge energy of young people, to encourage their developing skills, and to withstand what may be a healthy rebellion. Some children living in dire circumstances are unable to reach their potential because their family cannot fully support them in doing so - at an emotional as well as a financial level.

However, there are many parents who will fight for better prospects for their children and stretch out to grasp the best opportunities for them – perhaps with a little encouragement. Sue Gerhardt, a psychotherapist, who wrote The Selfish Society states in her book, *'Some parents who live in poverty will be able to withstand the impact of a stressful life because they have sufficient emotional resilience and confidence in others' helpfulness. They may be able to protect their children by passing on a sense of secure attachment…'* In other words, in creating strong roots they may be able to encourage their children to feel assured within themselves, to accept that they deserve more, to ask for help and to reach for their dreams.

When a parent believes *'I am a valuable person'*, he or she is more likely to pass on that message of self-confidence to the young ones. Furthermore, people from all ages are more likely to seek some backing if a system developed for the purpose of supporting families is in place in the community. As the statutory institutions can be viewed with much suspicion and fear, it is important to many of the families here that such an organisation of support is seen as different and (to a degree) separate from them.

As Richard Wilkinson and Kate Pickett, the authors of The Spirit Level (Why Equality is Better for Everyone) affirm, *'Because most of our abilities are learned, we depend on others for the acquisition of our life skills.'* Initially, we gain that knowledge from our parents. Later, if we want to change the direction of our lives, most of us need suggestions and feedback on how to advance; as well as requiring support from others while we are seeking new experiences. Altering our viewpoint on life rarely happens in isolation.

TRANSFORMING OUTLOOKS

Coming under the title of Future Families is Valleys Kids' most recent development of supporting families, designed to help them find the inner resources to lift their circumstances. Starting in 2010 and arising from the collective low self-esteem that is linked to the continuing dearth of jobs in this area, this project evolved from listening to many different members of the community. The business plan of this innovative scheme states: *'The Future Families programme has grown out of consultation with other service providers and statutory agencies in Rhondda Cynon Taf, our own experience through our work on a daily basis and discussion with the unemployed.'*

A well-planned and evolving programme, the goal is to reach out to those most at risk from being excluded from employment: those who were not able to respond positively to the education system; and those whose past experiences have created barriers, hindering them from accessing formal education or training within a statutory establishment. Many of the families being considered in this chapter are now in their second and sometimes third generation of unemployment. In such entrenched circumstances, the motivation to summon up the energy to change can be elusive. Encouraging people (with this life experience) into the workplace has to start at the most basic point, helping them believe that they have worth and that they have something to offer the community in which they live.

For Valleys Kids, Future Families work is a more structured way of working with the family as a complete unit. Centred in a Valleys Kids' Community Centre in the core of the neighbourhood, away from the schools, colleges or job centres, the buildings and ethos of Valleys Kids create an atmosphere of encouragement for those involved in this new project. The Future Families programme is an integral part of that centre. In-house staff members are involved in the training and support, along with those from the family team. Participants are provided with fresh opportunities for personal, familial and educational growth. The purpose is to provide a complementary system that helps to improve and upgrade different capabilities for the benefit of each and everyone in the family. As well as having a more harmonious family life, the hope is that through raising self-esteem and upgrading skills, the parents will feel positive enough to engage in further training or enter into employment.

It has been a deliberate decision to focus the family issues in this programme from the viewpoint of confidence building. This approach endorses parents by helping them acknowledge they have some of the answers to the issues surrounding their children, already. If they can't find the solution, they are encouraged to reach out and ask for help and to believe they have the right to do that. So many parenting classes have been thrust upon the recipients, so many mums and dads have felt talked down to and judged as bad parents - reinforcing inhibitions and the belief that they are not good enough.

*'I want to change.
I can change. I will
change.'*

A PROCESS OF CHANGE

In keeping with the philosophy of Valleys Kids and in
response to the impasse in which families find themselves,
the innovative work of Future Families has become an
established part of Valleys Kids. Along with colleagues
from the different projects, the Family Training team makes
use of behavioural change methods and skills to help
encourage and support the process of change. They are
trained in a technique called the Motivational Interviewing
Approach. This recognised good practice of intervention
predicts the changing phases and attitudes that occur in
the movement towards altering ingrained behaviours.
According to the book 'A Toolkit for Motivational Skills'
by Catherine Fuller and Phil Taylor, the progression of
adjusting one's thinking pursues the following stages and
pattern: *'I want to change. I can change. I will change.'*

In helping people work out what it is they want, while
not imposing opinions or rules, this method requires the
facilitator to establish a rapport with the service user;
to have well-developed listening skills; to ask proficient
questions which help keep the motivation going; to support
the person while they work through the changes they have
chosen and to have an understanding that change is a
process that takes time. During this procedure, most people
fluctuate in their attitude towards change. Sometimes they
can be excited about the new possibilities; sometimes they
are fearful of the unknown; sometimes there is a sequence
of elation as they discover fresh ways to deal with problems
and sometimes they feel stuck in the rut of ambivalence or
indecision. Ongoing support through the different phases
comes from the group work and regular meetings between
individual families and members of staff.

The Confident Kids: Confident Families groups are part

of the Future Families initiative and designed for families where the children are 5 to 11 years olds. The initial programme supports about 10 families for a ten weeks period. However, in recognising how deeply this collective low self-esteem is lodged, Valleys Kids acknowledges the need for sustained and ongoing support. When required, parents and children continue to be helped on an open-ended basis within the community centres.

Most of the referrals to this programme come from Children's Services, the largest majority come under the auspices of Child Protection. The presenting issue is usually a behavioural problem of one or more of the children. Initially, most families come because they want to fix the child. As Kath, the coordinator of this project mentions: *'What they learn is that if you want to change someone's behaviour, you have to start with you.'* As part of that adjustment, parents who attend find they have time and space to focus on themselves. Thus starting to change the steps and rhythm of the dance of the parent/child relationship and taking the intense spotlight off the child who acts out, for a while. As a consequence, adults can find themselves facing some of their own personal issues rather than displacing the entire family problem on to the child.

The Valleys Kids Community Centres provide a good catchment area for other mums and dads (usually mums) who want to engage in this confidence-building project. The parents in these groups tend to have younger children than the one mentioned above. Heather, who is the Future Family support worker has been establishing contact with groups that already exist, discussing what they would like to do to upgrade their skills or uplift their self-confidence. Some are considering a Cooking on a Budget course, others want to build their confidence through fitness and want to pursue exercise groups or Zumba, while others would like to train and gain qualifications in childcare.

I met with a group of mums in Penygraig; all of them single parents, all of them wanting to find work. Hannah, Hayley, Clare, Ria and Laura have all been trying to find employment, *'but there is nothing much around'*. If anything does come up, it rarely fits in with school hours making it impossible for them to take on the job. In the meantime through Future Families, they have been practicing being interviewed for a possible post, among other credentials they have gained their level one certificate in Food and Hygiene, they have become involved in voluntary work with the afterschools club and they have had *'chats about family'*. Prior to my meeting with them, one mum had discussed with Kath how best to handle some issues that might come up in a parents' evening in school. She said, *'It was like talking to a friend.'*

Throughout the book, I have described the relationship between staff of Valleys Kids and service users as a *'professional friendship.'* A reciprocal relationship is important to establish trust, to set up a rapport, to create a mutual respect. I have emphasized this important link as essential to the ability to hear clearly and to the need to support people through change. What is equally important in this relationship is the term 'professional.' For a Community Development Worker (whether working with family or with young people only), the professional part of that liaison comes from a background of relevant qualifications, ongoing training and support; from working within the clear ethos of Valleys Kids; from having a recognised evaluation programme set up to measure outcomes and effectiveness; from regularly reviewing all of the aforementioned and from holding the delicate balance between the 2 positions of being professional

and being a friend. The combination of those two roles demands a belief in the need for equality and the ability to be approachable while maintaining a professional distance. Yet, it also requires the self-assurance to not hide behind the front of being 'an expert', while being very skilled in this approach.

Kath and Heather were very clear that the comparative ease in which they have built up a trust and rapport with the different individuals and families is because they have no enforcement role. Their task is to listen to what the group members want, to draw opinions out. Heather commented, *'they are so used to attending the job centre. It took them a long time to realize that we weren't going to make them do anything they didn't want to do.'*

STRIKING A DIFFERENT CHORD

The blame game which surrounds decades of unemployment would have us believe that those who don't work are lazy, are spongers on state benefits and will do anything to avoid employment. To the staff of this initiative, this is a myth. Their evidence is that the work that is evolving from Future Families is growing very quickly. Their reality is that the adults and children with whom they are engaging are *'prolific consumers of new experiences.'* The parents want to try something new, they want to upgrade their skills, they want to build their confidence and they want to improve family life. There is enthusiasm for change. The challenge for society, for Valleys Kids, as well as the parents, is to keep that keenness alive in the present economic climate when jobs are few and far between.

In the meantime, families are preparing themselves in the hope that circumstances will get better. Also, they are learning to change some of the patterns of behaviour that have kept low their families' morale and aspirations. I asked the mums whom I interviewed if they thought that their attending the Future Family groups and getting help for themselves was benefiting their children. The reply was, **'Of course. If you are confident, the kids are more confident. We are their role models.'**

PART FOUR

Courses of
Communication

CHAPTER 10

Heeding the Tug of Curiosity

'Just as the body requires food for physical development and just as an appropriate balanced diet is essential for normal growth, so new experiences are needed for the mind.'

Dr Mia Kellmer Pringle wrote this in her book The Needs of Children. Originally published in 1975 and subsequently in 1980 and 1986, her document was written in reponse to a request by the Department of Social Security who wished to understand the developmental needs of children. Dr Pringle asserts that this need for new experiences and expanding knowledge continues throughout life. Mastering the ability to learn from life brings joy and a sense of achievement. She also emphasizes that if denied the opportunity of new experiences, learning for all ages becomes restricted. Therefore potential is buried, abilities are stunted - particularly for the young.

This need for being stimulated by the outside world appears to be just as important today in the 21st century as it was 3 or 4 decades ago. Over the years, there have been huge governmental campaigns to raise awareness about the importance of improving diet and exercise. As far as I am aware, there has been little publicity about the need for new experiences. Yet, according to a Save the Children report (2011), *'Children in severe poverty are*

'We have no television here. Our mobiles don't work here. It's great. We have to get on with other things.'

missing out on things like school trips and hobbies, hitting their educational and social development and leaving them excluded from society.'

The majority of young people have a natural curiosity, a yen to explore, and an urge to enquire. When encouraged to grow, that desire produces a powerful drive to learn. Nurturing that inquisitiveness is what helps them to grow in self-respect and self-confidence. In turn, that leads them to pushing boundaries and *'expanding their horizons.'*

New experiences can happen through different activities but little excites the mind as much as moving out of familiar territory. In their bid to help raise aspirations, Valleys Kids aims to encourage users of its service to take part in as many new experiences as possible.

EXPERIENCING, EXPLORING, EXPERIMENTING, EXPANDING

'We have no television here. Our mobiles don't work here. It's great. We have to get on with other things.'

This enthusiastic statement about adapting and trying a different approach came from 2 young volunteers from Penygraig Community Centre – Jordan (aged 13 and his friend Cameron aged 14 years). I met them on an away-day at Little Bryn Gwyn, Valleys Kids residential project in the Gower peninsula, near Swansea. On that particular day, they were there as part of a 'thank-you trip' for having looked after the younger ones during a summer play scheme. Both talked extensively about previous experiences when they had stayed overnight at this quiet retreat. In their eyes, each time, each visit had been 'an adventure'.

This special day's outing had been arranged as part of the Fresh Beginnings project for young people of 12 years and under. Three busloads of children from all Valleys Kids projects poured out onto the fields. Surrounding the house were (among other structures), a food tent, a bouncy castle, along with different canopies sheltering several artists who were demonstrating and organising a variety of craft activities. A man on stilts was wandering around, engaging with the kids and then was showing them how to make animals from balloons later. Hexagonal frames were being transformed into little houses by groups of young people with random pieces of material. Most of the children had dived into the dressing up box. With their faces painted as butterflies or animals of some kind and wearing imaginative outfits, they looked resplendent.

A caterer had donated a huge 'palm tree' whose trunk was covered with chunks of fresh fruit secured to the tree with cocktail sticks. It was placed in the conservatory of Little Bryn Gwyn. Fascinated youngsters constantly surrounded this display, persistently picking away at the fruit and devouring huge quantities. The noise levels and amount of excited running around coming from the garden and fields suggested they were all having great fun. It was a day of exploring, experimenting and gaining from new experiences.

On the previous week, I had visited Flightwings, part of the ArtWorks project, who were down there at Little Bryn Gwyn for a couple of nights. Although this is an older group, the atmosphere was just as charged, just as excited, if a little sleepier because of late nights. They worked on their drama in the morning and escaped to the beach in the afternoon. Over the summer several had been involved in volunteer work with the different younger groups belonging to the ArtWorks department. The purposes of this visit were

to have a break from that hard work, to recharge batteries and to have time to prepare themselves for future shows: to learn, to bond and to improve their skills.

During my various conversations with different age groups I found that this retreat is well used and well loved by many members of Valleys Kids. The time and space away from 'normal life' were much appreciated by all age groups. There are plans to make it even more popular, to bring new exciting activities to more young people and their families, in the future.

LITTLE BRYN GWYN

The importance of taking kids away from their local area in small groups was recognised early on in the history of the Penygraig Community Project. When I interviewed some of the first members of the Bike Club they still had very clear memories of those experiences that happened over 30 years ago. Some of the original youthworkers remember taking groups of about 10 youngsters to Bala in North Wales. There, professional outdoor pursuits people trained them in demanding activities. Together, youthworkers and kids learned the skills of canoeing, rock-climbing and gorge walking. When people are thrown into such a challenging situation where they have to help each other to survive, the benefits are all about confidence building, establishing trust and working as a team. For a while, PCP also took small groups to Brechfa in Carmarthenshire to a very basic residential place with no inside toilet and a concrete floor. Despite the meagre conditions, those who took part enjoyed different games, walks in the forest, and mastering different survival skills. The learning experiences that emerged from these activities sowed the seeds of dreams for Valleys Kids about owning their own 'hostel' somewhere outside the valleys.

Little Bryn Gwyn, the place that eventually met that fantasy, started its history as a farmhouse. The property is fairly remote, off the road, hidden from passers-by, allowing for the opportunity to make as much noise as possible while not upsetting the neighbours. As well as the house and outbuildings, there are 2 sizeable fields that can be used for camping and other activities.

The 10th newsletter for Valleys Kids, published in Spring 2004, celebrates with the following words. 'After many long months of fundraising and optimistic thinking Valleys Kids is now the proud owner of Little Bryn Gwyn.' Previously, Valleys Kids had leased this property from Barnados for the purpose of giving small groups of young people the opportunity to sample residential periods away from home, filled with adventure. In March 2003 the organisation was given first refusal to purchase the small farm. Recognising and valuing the many positive experiences that this little house provided for the children and young people of Rhondda Cynon Taf, Valleys Kids did not refuse. Huge energy went in to raising the funds to be able to purchase this property. Generous donations from local individuals and businesses helped make this possible.

In order to upgrade and refurbish Little Bryn Gwyn even further, much hard work continues in raising funds for this project. The management and fundraising team's long-term goal is to create a more beautiful, environmentally friendly 'eco-learning' retreat for children and families. Predominantly used by Valleys Kids people, the property is occasionally let out to other agencies. While the staff team plans to hold on to the major share of lettings, it is working towards being more available to other interested parties in the future.

THE OPENING OF OPPORTUNITIES

Various members from the different Valleys Kids projects shared their opinions of Little Bryn Gwyn. For several, this haven is special because it gives opportunities of first experience. Jordan and Cameron were introduced to *'stuff we wouldn't do normally,'* like rock-climbing with a qualified instructor. Another novel activity for some youthful residents is involvement in the planning of menus and helping prepare the meals. For a number of young people it was a new experience to sit down as a group and eat together, making meals into social occasions. Some families had their first holiday together here, as a unit. A group of mums were planning an experimental break away from the children in Little Bryn Gwyn. Many of the younger generation experienced their initial overnight trip away from home. This included a young woman (aged 23 years) with whom I met during a visit there. As with some of the other visitors, moving out of what is familiar and leaving family was a major step for her to take.

Talk to kids about their experience of Little Bryn Gwyn and inevitably 4 major activities are dominant in the conversation. Walks in the woods at midnight when listening to scary ghost stories are mentioned frequently. Other favourite topics are sitting around the campfire, sleeping (or not) in the barn and finally, going to the beach. Alternative activities are important too but traditionally these come top of the list – not necessarily in the order given.

The seclusion and environs of this outdoor centre lend themselves to being a safe place for free play, where young people can indulge in imaginative games with no interference from organising adults. They (the grown-ups) know when to keep an eye on proceedings from a distance.

More organised fun is arranged at other times of the day. There are trees to climb; there is a lot of space where they can run around. As well as bringing much enjoyment, the freedom to explore and to play can offer a valuable learning experience. It is a time when kids may learn to assert themselves, to negotiate with each other, while being quite creative and inventive. Mia Kellner Pringle sums up the advantages of this recreation. *'Play can be seen to meet the need for new experiences in two major ways: by enabling the child to learn about the world he lives in; and by providing a means for learning about and resolving complex and often conflicting emotions.'*

Another advantage of a residential break to this quiet place is that by its very nature it involves working with small groups only. This gives the children opportunities to bond together more closely and it provides the youthworkers with time to get to know the young ones better. Sometimes, hectic youth club evenings in the home area don't allow staff to allocate much time to individuals or small groups of kids. Days and nights spent at Little Bryn Gwyn help counteract that busyness, giving precious time to listen, to hear in more detail what it is that young people want to say and to prepare the ground for such times when they might want to reach out and ask for help. Often, the close relationships mentioned in other chapters evolve here. Caroline, a youth worker from Penyrenglyn was quoted in the previously mentioned newsletter as saying: *'coming here gives us (youth workers) the opportunity to work with young people away from their day-to-day environment. That kind of interaction is invaluable to our work.'*

It has been a deliberate policy not to have a television set at Little Bryn Gwyn. This, along with the fact that the farm is situated in a 'black hole' for mobile phones, adds to the atmosphere of being free from the distractions of present

'Valleys Kids takes us out of the Rhondda. We need to get out of the Rhondda to meet other people, see different things and know about other ways of life.

day technological gadgets, for a short while. Connected to the outside world by a landline when necessary, the groups are free to experience the natural silence and to take time to listen and communicate with each other.

For children, Little Bryn Gwyn is a place of fun and of exploration, a setting in which to bond with other people. Adults have had similar experiences there, too. However for them, it can be something more: a place in which to find some calmness and personal space. One woman, who had suffered great tragedy and loss in her life, visited with a Feeling Good group for a day. She said little while she was there except to repeat often, 'it is so peaceful here.' The isolation and quietness of Little Bryn Gwyn gave her just what she needed - a much-needed break from the ongoing tension in her life. Time away offered her the opportunity to gather energy that would help her face the troubles at home.

STEPPING OUT OF THE VALLEYS

During an interview, one girl said, *'Valleys Kids takes us out of the Rhondda. We need to get out of the Rhondda to meet other people, see different things and know about other ways of life. My auntie has rarely left the street she lives in. That is her life. All she does is talk about the man next door. I want more than that.'* Other young people repeated this comment in different ways.

Circumstances in life can help curb people's dreams and stifle their curiosity to explore. Leaving the confines of the village or township can be a challenge for some people living in Rhondda Cynon Taf. For example, one mum who attended a parent support group had not travelled as far as Cardiff (12 miles from her home) for over 10 years.

Sometimes, for some individuals and families the restriction of travel is caused by ill health. (She suffered from many years of depression). Her story is not unusual. Others cannot move far because they are unable to afford the rail or bus travel. Often, social occasions such as going to see a show or meeting friends at a club are limited by transport timetables that do not accommodate late night jaunts. Occasionally, fear of the unknown keeps people tied to the boundaries of their home area, their comfort zone.

When Valleys Kids talks of *'broadening horizons'* it does not mean in a psychological manner, only. Its approach is a practical one. In order to help young people and adults have wider visions of what is possible, the organisation provides a channel of new experiences that require looking outside their village. At times, this includes stepping out of the valleys to learn about life in other communities, in other countries and in other parts of the world. Broadening our outlook brings so much self-confidence, helps in our understanding of other ways of life, while opening up new prospects. Claire from Chapter 8 described a trip to Birmingham with ArtWorks. As well as widening their experience in drama, this excursion gave the young people the opportunity to meet individuals from different backgrounds. For the first time, it introduced the group to people who are black. The South Wales valleys do not have many residents belonging to different ethnicities. Claire commented, *'It helped the boys see that they are just the same as us really. It helped take away prejudice.'*

Trips to a theatre to see a show, to sports venues to watch a rugby match; journeys to partake in sponsored bike rides in West Wales or to sail in the Bristol Channel and tours to beaches within easy reach like Barry or Porthcawl: these are all examples of some of the away from home experiences. Occasionally, just taking the kids out of their

neighbourhood to visit one of the other areas coming under the Valleys Kids umbrella widens social circles and brings new friendships. Joint excursions, where members of 2 or 3 community centres travel to a similar project in Aberdeenshire or even further afield to Prague to experience a different approach to youthwork also gives participants new understanding when learning about other cultures. Often the experience is positive, but sometimes it may bring some challenges such as being confronted by homesickness. Disturbing as that is, learning to manage that overwhelming feeling presents a new challenge too.

It is often said that travelling broadens the mind. At times, it can take us into situations of great anxiety. Through Valleys Kids a small number of young people have taken long trips to other continents like Africa and America. Imagine the courage it takes for a young person from a really close community like Mount Libinus in Penyrenglyn to board the long flight to New York. Then, to take part in a summer camp in the United States where the greatest majority of the participants come from very privileged backgrounds. Envisage how it lifts self-esteem when you have been brought up in an area which did not enjoy a good reputation and you discover that you can hold your own with someone from a different culture, someone who has had an easier start in life. Consider how that changes mindsets. See how aspirations can grow and what new possibilities appear, as a result.

LEARNING TO SING IN HARMONY

Learning from other cultures does not always require travelling away from home. On occasion, the outside world comes to the Rhondda bringing more rich and life-enhancing experiences.

As well as encouraging individuals and families to widen horizons, Valleys Kids as an organisation has chosen to broaden its vision too, and embarked on a huge international project through the Cultural Olympiad. Culminating in the year 2012, along with 4 other Welsh cultural projects, this nation-wide initiative celebrated the London Olympic and Paralympic Games through the arts. All 5 projects were supported under the umbrella of the Legacy Trust UK.

Valleys Kids involvement with this ambitious venture arose largely through an interest to link with townships in South Africa. It was built on the arts, but was fundamentally about developing the relationship between two cultures for mutual benefit, then and in the future. Fundraiser Denise Lord coordinates this project that has been entitled Mzansi Cymru. As we know, Cymru is the Welsh name for Wales. Mzansi is a local slang word for South Africa. The joint heading symbolises a combined celebration of the communities in South Wales and the townships in Capetown. The tribute marks what they have in common: a passion for the arts and a similar history in mining, as well as a first hand experience of differing degrees of deprivation.

The juxtaposition of the two cultures brought them together to celebrate in *an epic piece of musical theatre',* an intercultural play written by playwright Larry Allan. The plot of the drama, placed within the making of the film Zulu, embraces both ways of life. The ambition was to invite a percussion, song and dance band; a young peoples' choir; a circus and a dance company from South Africa to unite with people from Rhondda Cynon Taf and perform this play, alongside each other.

As part of the research for this book, seeking information on how Valleys Kids impacts on young peoples' lives, I met with the Welsh section of the choir to learn what being involved in the artistic adventure of Mzansi Cymru meant to them. What first impressed me was the diversity of people within the group. Just under 30 individuals attended choir practice. They represented all ages and came from many walks of life, travelling in from different parts of the county.

My next recollection of the atmosphere of the group was the sense of togetherness. There was an air of joint commitment, accompanied by a feeling of combined pleasure in the singing. Some of the tunes were traditional. With input from the members of the choir, composer and musical director Paula Gardiner had created new songs. One young woman, with obvious choral and musical talent, relieved Paula from leading the group for a while and led the choir through different harmonies. To my untrained ear, the collective sound they made was beautiful and impressive.

Unexpectedly, when I arrived, I was greeted at the door by 4 of the lads whom I knew from the Pen Dinas Youth group, who were eager to tell me of what they had achieved, generally. In particular, they wanted to share what they had gained through their involvement in the choir. As you may remember from previous pages, the Pen Dinas estate has a history of being excluded from the wider community. It has taken several years of the boys being involved in new learning experiences with both Penygraig and Pen Dinas Community Projects to reach this stage of confidence, to have a belief in their skills and talents. (They are now in their mid to late teens.)

They had just been informed that a video (which had been made to herald the forthcoming Cultural Olympiad across the UK) had been released to go nationwide. Guided by Larry and rapper Clayton George, their input to this, which included performances of rap, had been chosen to represent Wales in the short film. Also, one of the boys was being encouraged to develop his obvious talent at playing the keyboard. As I participated in the choir practice and observed, I could see they were very much at ease in the company of the mixed group, enjoying the joint activity, feeling included and rightfully, very proud of their contribution. One of the more grey-haired members of the choir informed me that when they first started attending he didn't think they would last. However, they have been attending choir practice regularly every Thursday evening for more than two years, and taken part in different concerts. All 4 boys have become an integral part of this venture.

Their experience of working as part of a close team, and of 'releasing their creativity' expanded extensively. After the break, a different video was shown of how the South African contribution to this show was developing. What became clear from watching that massive production was that this group of Welsh singers was to merge with Fezeka Voice to create one mass choir for the performance of the musical play. As I mingled with the members during the break, one young woman of about 16 years commented, 'now we will have to up our game!' What she was predicting is that talents and skills will be stretched to their fullest capacity. This is an extraordinary choir from Fezeka High School, in Cape Town, which educates children from the deprived backgrounds of the townships. They are renowned internationally for their outstanding musical ability.

'The aim in youth work is to enable young people to grow and develop, to grow in self-respect and confidence which helps them achieve their potential.'

The publication proclaiming the final performance of this musical states: *'the prestigious Donald Gordon Stage will see this epic spectacle come to fruition in a co-production with the Wales Millennium Centre.'* Performing in this iconic theatre under these circumstances provided a new learning experience of huge proportions, for all involved. The combination of voices made a very powerful statement of unity through this multi-cultural experience.

ACHIEVING POTENTIAL

The Way Ahead, Valleys Kids strategic plan of 2013 -2016 states that its aim in youth work *'is to enable young people to grow and develop, to grow in self-respect and confidence which helps them achieve their potential.'* One of the tools, which goes a long way to helping them achieve this goal, is the provision of new and challenging experiences. Creating stimulating environments is part of the capacity building approach of the organisation. This attitude occurs across the board, in all of the Community Centres; in ArtWorks; in Family Training; in Playwork and in Mzansi Cymru. All parts of the organisation are united in that aim of drawing out innate inquisitiveness.

So many young people have had their natural curiosity dampened down through low expectations, poor financial resources and low self-esteem, in the past. Valleys Kids have brought a fresh approach to stimulating that inborn need to explore. Learning from situations away from home, from other locations, bringing in new groups or cultures are essential components of this method, conveying new perspectives and new outlooks on life.

Summing up the lessons learned in this chapter as communicated by the young people involved, the embracing of new experiences has brought the following returns:

- Knowledge of survival skills;
- New relationships with all age groups;
- New social skills;
- Learning different approaches to life;
- The development of musical and artistic abilities;
- Information on other areas in this country and abroad;
- An understanding of different cultures;
- Discovering methods of how to plan and work out different problems;
- Finding ways to operate in a small group;
- Enjoyment of the environment;
- An introduction to different outdoor pursuits.

Above all, they have had fun, they have been stimulated, they have had the courage to do something differently and they have had great pleasure in finding out more about who they are and what they are capable of doing.

Keep in mind that some of these kids are among the most challenged. Sometimes they can be amongst the most challenging, too. What I think they are telling us is: given the right encouragement and circumstances, they have huge potential, individually and collectively. That has to be acknowledged, nourished and respected, for the benefit of us all. They have much to teach us if we are prepared to really listen.

CHAPTER 11

Amplifying the Sense of Community

'Going to Wales to take part in Torchbearers helped me realise that it is not only South African youth that are going through tough times. I met some of the young people from the South Wales valleys and saw where they lived. They have it tough too. Like me, they are not ashamed of where they come from. Together, we share a passion for the arts and we have these shared dreams that will help us win through.'

This succinct appraisal came from Nathan (aged 20). He is one of the dancers from the Dance For All team from Cape Town, South Africa. He performed in the huge cultural exchange scheme created by Valleys Kids in collaboration with several arts based projects from South Wales and some others set up to help young people from the townships (which are part of greater Cape Town.)

Nathan explained that his home is in a rural area where gangsters wield much power. *'The arts help me not to succumb to their demands.'* Wisely, he acknowledged that not everyone would win through, but thought that with such purpose, many would. Other members of the Dance For All team, Tamsyn (17) and Vuva (16) agreed that among the many advantages of their love for dance was that it gave them a focus, kept them off the streets and helped them avoid the ever present temptations of alcohol and drugs.

They had discovered innate creative abilities and friendship: two very powerful tools to help them push off into a successful existence.

Initially, Nathan identifying with our local boys surprised me. I have written much about the effects of poverty on children in Wales but the return visit to Cape Town put into sharp focus the different degrees of adversity that people living in the townships have to endure. There is no comparison. Many children growing up in South Africa have a much more difficult start in life than their Welsh peers. My interpretation of what he was recognising was the sliding scale of injustice that prevails because of the international distribution of wealth, causing many young people in both countries to start their lives with different levels of disadvantage.

On the other hand, he was also acknowledging that these particular youngsters from both continents had found some fortune. They had discovered innate creative abilities and friendship: two very powerful tools to help them push off into a successful existence. Also, they had been given opportunities to develop both. This initiative of Mzansi Cymru is a part of that chance to change direction in life.

Mzansi Cymru is the name of the artistic and collaborative project discussed in this chapter. This international partnership between Wales and South Africa was part of the Cultural Olympiad, which ran in parallel to the Olympic games in 2012. The focus of the exchange was a musical extravaganza called Torchbearers, a fictional love story set in the time of apartheid. That narrative brought together 2 diverse cultures from different continents to celebrate their similarities: a history of mining, the challenge of living in marginalised communities and a love of the arts. The shows were presented and performed in both Cardiff and Cape Town.

The experience of sharing this massive and inspired project has opened up many supportive relationships between young people in South Africa and the South Wales valleys. Those feelings of togetherness, those continuing connections that grew from collaborating in a joint project arising from shared interests and experiences have been intensified and prolonged with the aid of Facebook. Communication between the young men and women from the 2 different continents continues.

CREATING A COMMUNITY OF GREATER CAPACITY

Historically, the mining communities of the valleys are renowned for a strong neighbourhood bond. The townships of South Africa have a similar reputation. Sadly, the infrastructure supporting communities in both countries is slowly being eroded by economics, causing the subsequent need for migration. It would be easy to sit back and take that sense of community for granted or to deny it is under attack. It is important to find alternative ways to help that supportive system survive.

I hope that one of the main messages that thrusts its way through the pages of this book is that if we are to help strengthen the wings and roots of young people, we must encourage them to develop a strong sense of community. Also, we must help them be aware of that positive force standing alongside them, supporting the development of who they are and wanting the best for their future. This is what Valleys Kids strives to create and promote through a two way process of give and take.

Valleys Kids has been engaged in international projects before. Yet, although rooted in the same ethics and aiming for the same objectives and although the project involved a number of young people and staff from the organisation, Mzansi Cymru was different in its approach, mainly in scale and pace. Usually, by its very nature, community development work evolves. Shaped by the people involved, it moves at their rhythm and is determined by their drive and the availability of finance. Often, it starts quite small before it grows into something much larger.

The bringing together of the Torchbearers' story, the creating of bridges between organisations in South Africa and Wales, the melding of different artistic mediums was hugely ambitious and brave. Along with the main actors, the organisers of Mzansi Cymru merged the creative talents of 14 different specialist groups. Seven of those teams came from South Africa, seven from Wales. All organisations were dedicated to a branch of the arts and all were committed to helping improve the lives of young people. For the production in Cardiff Millennium Centre, July 2012, the cast of actors, dancers and acrobats along with the orchestra, choirs and production crew consisted of over 150 people. Backing them up was a large team of volunteers and advisors.

The size and time scale demanded a more authoritative approach than the method of the ArtWorks team and the youth workers of Valleys Kids. Yet, despite the preliminary work occurring simultaneously in 2 different continents; regardless of size and differences in culture and language; even with time and finance dictating that the complete team spent only 4 weeks of a 5 year period together (2 weeks in Cardiff and 2 in Cape Town) many of the participants found a powerful sense of solidarity and community.

Laurence Allan, writer and artistic director of Torchbearers confirms that one of the intentions of the production of this musical play was to celebrate the sense of loyalty and engagement of these different communities; also, to rejoice

'It taught me a lot about trust. It was like being in another family.'

in a connection between the two. Indeed, he saw the collaboration as much more important than the piece. His writing produced a strong story giving opportunity to bring together physically, members of the different international neighbourhoods, honouring the 2 cultures and histories.

' I connected with Mzansi Cymru immediately. I felt part of a unit. I had never been out of South Africa before. It was exciting and scary. When we changed planes in Amsterdam I lost my cell phone. I panicked. I felt cut off from my friends and family. I felt alone. When we arrived in Cardiff the boys told Denise of my problem. Everyone was very kind and helped me stay in touch with those back home. It taught me a lot about trust. It was like being in another family.'

This was part of Mandisa's story of her involvement in the production of Torchbearers. Mandisa was 20 when she came here to participate with her peers from Zip Zap Circus. She is a highly skilled acrobat. For large parts of the show she moved elegantly, with great ease on large hoops and swathes of material, high above us giving visual impact to the unfolding story.

I make use of her experience to illustrate the transition that people made coming in from the security of their own groups and neighbourhoods to a much larger community which was international in nature: the phenomenon of Mzansi Cymru. Also, I borrow her words to highlight the fellowship that people may feel even in very large groups when they share a similar cause.

CAPTURING THE ESSENCE OF COMMUNITY

I pondered the vastness and complexities of this particular project that had all sorts of different offshoots, and so many partners, collaborators and supporters. I wondered how I was going to keep it simple enough to capture the essence, the importance of the feeling of kinship and support. I questioned how I would portray the expansion of the concept of community to something much more widespread than the confines of local neighbourhoods.

Other publications cover the enormity and scale of this project in a much more comprehensive way than I can. Other mediums have highlighted the work of some of the key people: directors and main actors. In the context of this book, my role is not to comment on the artistic merit, wonderful as it was. My role is as a researcher exploring the impact of Valleys Kids' community work projects on the lives of some of the people involved.

In order to draw on some external expertise and insight, I have chosen to lean on two closely related philosophies:

- The findings of a paper named Psychological Sense of Community: A Definition and Theory written by McMillan and Chavis.
- The wisdom of the South African value of Ubuntu

I will consider the latter first.

UBUNTU

Perhaps the best summing up of the sense of community integral to the culture of Valleys Kids and to the huge

'I am what I am because of who we all are.'

creative adventure of Mzansi Cymru comes from the South African word ubuntu. As well as producing the ideal that the artistic project worked towards, this visualisation was the container of so many diverse groups and talents. It was the glue that held things together.

It is believed by some that it is the essence of ubuntu that continues to help the recovering nation of South Africa in easing the healing after the ravages of apartheid. It means: *'I am what I am because of who we all are.'* In the preface to a book named Mandela's Way - Lessons on Life, the subject of the study (Nelson Mandela) clarifies the definition further: *'In Africa, there is a concept known as ubuntu - the profound sense that we are human only through the humanity of others; that if we are to accomplish anything in this life, it will in equal measure be due to the work and achievements of others.'* Essential to the practice of Ubuntu is the ethos of respect for and responsibility to others, requiring the ability to listen well. Necessary to this philosophy is an attitude of equality, mutuality and reciprocity.

I have to admit that while I am writing this particular chapter, I am wearing two hats: one professional and the other intensely personal. In previous pages, I describe visiting the Welsh intergenerational community choir that (along with the musical ensemble and original jazzy music) provided an anchor for the story of Torchbearers. I did that for the purposes of research but I was so intrigued by what I found there, I returned and still attend the choir in the aftermath of the Mzansi Cymru project.

While I have no particular talent for singing, I enjoy it. What gives me greater pleasure is the sense of community, the harmony, the melding of different voices to produce a collective and beautiful sound and rhythm. I come out of each choir practice or performance on a high. My sense of well-being blossoms from that interdependence, the supporting of each other to 'up our game' by doing the best we can.

From the perspective of the choir, that security which came from a smallish group of about 30 people was challenged, suddenly. As the South Africans flew into Cardiff, the 'team' mushroomed into a large international community. Although at times, I felt overwhelmed by the hugeness of it all, I experienced the benefits of being part of the whole extravaganza. It was an interlinking of many skills, many individuals and many groups each dependent on the other to create a united whole. The medium of different arts became a conduit for assembled voices shouting about the injustices of apartheid: unfairness, divisiveness and inequality – the dark side of humanity. Alternatively, it placed a spotlight on the effect of a juxtaposition of many facets of human creativity. It built bridges between diverse communities in dissimilar continents by helping individuals experience the different ways of living while celebrating and nurturing the similarities of those neighbourhoods.

It would be easy to paint a very romantic picture of the processing of these ideals. In fact, reality presented many challenges to the 'togetherness' of it all. For example, there was a long wait while decisions were made about government funding. If that had not materialised, the African teams would have withdrawn from the project. Also, securing visas for their visit provided a huge headache for Denise Lord who managed it all. Negotiations in merging the musical score with the script demanded time. Tensions existed between different groups. Some adults became irritated at the boisterousness of some young people; in Cardiff, some of the Welsh choir saw themselves as 'out on a limb'; some members of the musical ensemble

felt disrespected by other members of the orchestra and some of the Africans clung together in the security of their own group while wishing they had the experience of their compatriots in staying with Welsh families. A sense of community does not mean that there is no discord. It requires having a collective commitment to acknowledge those issues and work them through. It demands a generosity of spirit from all concerned while pushing towards a common goal.

Importantly, it all came together on the night. (It was six nights really – 3 in Cardiff in July and 3 in Cape Town in November). Problems were solved, people forgot or worked through their differences, and everyone upped their game, uniting in perfecting the performance, passing on the message of unification to warm and responsive audiences.

AN EXPERIENCE OF INTERNATIONAL COMMUNITY

McMillan and Chavis state that a Sense of Community is experiential and comes from a shared history. They believe: *'A sense of community is a feeling that members have of belonging, a feeling that members matter to one another and to the group, and a shared faith that members' needs will be met through their commitment to be together.'* They propose that it is composed of 4 elements:

Membership
Influence
Integration and Fulfilment of Needs
Shared emotional connection

I use these sub-headings to help understand and describe the sense of intercontinental community that arose from the Mzansi Cymru project. Although closely related, the subjects of Integration and Fulfilment of Need are so large and important I have decided to split the 2, creating 5 topics for discussion.

MEMBERSHIP.

Membership comes from a sense of belonging, which, in turn comes from feeling secure in what you are participating. For many of the participants, the atmosphere of safety was eased in that they already belonged to close-knit groups. There was an ambience of established friendship evident in their own genres. The challenges were in bringing the diverse groups together and in the experiences of cultural exchange. Shortness of time with each other was a major factor in pulling together the greater picture.

I met with groups from both countries to question them about this sense of community. In Wales, I interviewed people from the ArtWorks team (discussed in earlier chapters) and with members of the Mzansi Cymru choir and Extraordinary Ensemble. While in Cape Town my meetings took place with representatives from 3 of the agencies working to help young people from South Africa create a better life. Those groups were:

- Dance for All which was the vision of Philip Boyd and his wife, the late prima Ballerina Assoluta Phyllis Spira. It was created with the aim of providing children in historically disadvantaged communities with the opportunity for enjoyment and empowerment, promoting the growth of self-esteem through the medium of dance. Dance for All has also initiated a very successful programme to train young African people as professional dancers and are developing a unique indigenous dance company.

- Zip Zap Circus school was also set up by a husband and wife team Brent Van Rensburg and Laurence Esteve. It provides young people in Cape Town with opportunities to break the cycle of isolation and poverty. This enables them to be employable and contributing citizens of the new South Africa. This is all achieved through a variety of disciplines including trapeze work, unicycle riding, balancing feats, dancing, juggling, acrobatics, and comedy.

- Fezeka's Voice was developed in Fezeka High School in the township of Gugulethu under the leadership of Phumi Tsewu who was born and raised during the time of apartheid. He knows that one of the only ways for black South Africans to claim their right to a free and just society is to teach children they are worthy of it. The 20-strong choir have gained an international reputation and several have progressed to become professional singers.

Feeling safe was a matter of discussion for the young people from both continents.

The young women from Fezeka's Voice politely declined to give me an interview. Instead, some volunteered to write their thoughts down. Initially, they recorded this in their own language on their phones and then wrote it in English for me, on paper. They chose this method of communication as the one they were most comfortable with. Lungelwa, one of the group, appreciated the stability, consistency and the professionalism of the Welsh team.

'stepping so far out of our comfort zone – going where we knew nobody.'

She felt that, *'they give all the best in everything they do and they are prepared all the time.'* Another young woman, also called Fezeka (aged 18) talked of the *'kindness, caring and love'* she received in Wales. *'We didn't feel like foreigners,'* she added.

From the Welsh group, Steve a member of the ArtWorks team of Valleys Kids described his trip to South Africa as a *'stepping so far out of our comfort zone – going where we knew nobody.'* That involvement helped him appreciate both his *'safety net in the valleys'* and how much the African people went out of their way to make him feel comfortable. Several members of this set of young people shared that what they experienced in Cape Town had brought their own group closer together.

McMillan and Chavis say that the feeling of membership can be measured by the amount of commitment shown by different participants. Examples of the different degrees of engagement in this project are many. From the long battles of the coordinating staff in struggling with the bureaucracy of governments, in raising funding so this mission could happen - to the merging and fine-tuning of the script and the musical score. Added to this was the patient undertaking to blend the artistic expression of many groups.

One family in the Welsh party found that membership of Mzansi Cymru became a main focus of their lives over the 4 years. From the beginning, Mike, Hina, Olivia and Manisha committed themselves to this project at a high level. Olivia travelled its journey as far as the performances in Cardiff in July. The rest of the family were involved all the way through *'watching the jigsaw puzzle steadily take shape.'* Hina was a member of the Extraordinary Ensemble and with her talents in singing and playing the guitar, became one of the leaders of the choir. From the background, Mike supported the process too adopting several roles. Among them, he was an active member of the choir. Also, with experience in acting, he stood in when some of the main actors were unable to turn up for occasional rehearsals and was part of a group that met informally supporting the directors of the project as its enormity unfolded. Manisha was 9 going on 10 at the beginning of the project and aged 14 when she travelled to Cape Town. She looked forward to Thursday nights that were the regular choir practice time and to taking part in different workshops.

As with most participants, membership was rewarding, too. As a result of this experience, Hina's belief in her musical abilities has grown, encouraging her to make her own albums. Mike is more confident in his singing and is inspired to continue to develop that skill further. For Manisha, one of the benefits is that she has made several friends in Africa, as well as in Wales.

Several of the teams initiated different fundraising schemes to help the cultural exchange take place. Although their personal circumstances prevented them from travelling to Cape Town, some of the Welsh choir arranged a concert and a raffle in order to help others to go. Their attitude was, *'We wanted to do it because it was important.'* While all of the young people and cast were financed for this particular experience, many of the adults paid for travel and accommodation so that they could take part, too. ArtWorks raised £1500 towards their costs. Over a 4-year period, participants turned up for rehearsals week after week sometimes in not the most conducive of venues. (Sometimes the cold and poor acoustics raised some challenges!) However, there was a collective faith that the instigators of this project would bring it all together. That was achieved with the support of all of the teams involved. The high level of personal investment and commitment was obvious throughout the community.

INFLUENCE

'It is the ACTION of this disparate group of people all agreeing and doing something (almost impossible) together that I carry with me; each individual offering his or her own unique quality to the whole. It is from doing this together in pursuit of excellence that the cultural exchange/meeting grew in resonance, confidence and meaning. It is this that profoundly bonds and unites. It is this challenging yet celebratory experience and memory that both young and old will carry back to their respective countries and in so doing further nurture their own lives and cultures.'

I quote from a blog written by Phil McKenzie, Creative Director of Torchbearers. Retrospectively, this message sums up his experience with this project.

For a deep sense of community to exist, McMillan and Chavis argue that each member must experience a two-way process of influence. While the community encourages each member, they in turn must feel empowered to effect the whole. This requires balancing an atmosphere of trust that comes from the protective network of the shared ethics, expectations and goals of the community, while cherishing each individual's input.

So often, those who grow up in the valleys of South Wales and the townships of South Africa find themselves judged, ignored, dismissed, not listened to, devalued and discouraged by those who see themselves as separate or in a different class. Because of this experience young people can learn to see themselves as being of little value. Yet, as all the projects involved here prove over and over again the promise of these youngsters is huge.

The pioneers of Mzansi Cymru wanted to give all those involved a message to *'be proud of who you are'*: to treasure their history, circumstances and capabilities. The atmosphere of mutual friendship embedded in the arts project allowed this potential to flourish. The expectation that everyone would reach for excellence in their performance pushed them to believe in their creative abilities, in what they had to give.

One of the many stimuli that emanated from the African teams came from their high standard of professionalism. All of the afore-mentioned organisations that came from Cape Town had experience of performing on an international stage. All of their participants were trained to a highly proficient standard. On the other hand, the Welsh community choir had been brought together for the purposes of this project and the orchestra was a mixture of professional, semi-professional and enthusiastic amateurs. The ArtWorks team was used to performing but not on such prestigious stages as the Millennium Centre in Cardiff and Artscape in Cape Town. The challenge to all was to reach for the highest standard, to be seen as important as each other and to support each other in doing so.

Vuva (a representative of Dance for All) explained her passion for her art. Dance had helped her find a way of expressing how she feels. *'I have difficulty with words but I tell a different story with my body.'* Along with so many others, she had found a way of communicating, of being heard and in this case was honing her skill to help tell the story of apartheid from generations before. Her 'voice' joined the different artistic modes of expression, uniting as one to tell this tale. The languages of varied arts coming together in this way conveyed a powerful message. Each person had their own way of describing the picture and each individual brought their particular influence on the project. In turn, the support of the community impacted on the individual, helping them believe in their worth.

Mandisa of Zip Zap Circus described the thrill of being seen as an ambassador for her country. She had not anticipated that she was worthy of that honour. She was aware of her obvious and developing skills as an artist but until her visit to Wales had not appreciated that she had what it takes to be valued as a representative of her country. While she was conscious of what she had been given through the Mzansi Cymru experience, she was only becoming alert to her capacity to influence, gradually. That lesson did much for her self-esteem.

Members of the ArtWorks team were proud that they had given their best to the shows, raising their game with each one. However when I met with them, they were more tuned into what they had received from the project and from the Africans they met than what they had given. They had to be reminded of examples of their spirit of generosity in taking care of each other, in forming continuing friendships outside their immediate group and in helping some of the mums and the less able who struggled with the gruelling trip climbing down from Table Mountain. Their memories had to be refreshed about the comments that came from the hotel staff about their responsible behaviour. Their gifts of sensitivity, supportiveness and caring had to be reflected back to them, as had their willingness to be open-minded and to try new experiences from a different culture, like eating sheep's eyes and caterpillars!

Recognising and appreciating our ability to influence and affect other people as well as the wider picture, is a process that grows with self-esteem. Despite many young people from both countries being somewhat oblivious as to how they had stimulated the whole picture, their input was large. The positive sense of community was there and came from an expectation and ambience of give and take. The influence worked both ways.

INTEGRATION

If one word could be used to describe what was achieved in the Mzansi Cymru project it would be integration. The whole agenda was created to highlight that issue. The sensitive love story between a boy from the mining communities of South Wales and a young Zulu girl in the time of apartheid brought the matter into sharp focus. The powerful musical score that melded folk songs from both countries into a jazzy orchestration also brought about that atmosphere of amalgamation. Paula Gardiner, head of Jazz at the Royal Welsh Academy of Music and Drama, as well as composer and musical director of this show describes her vision: *'It became clear that the score was going to be performed by an ensemble of instruments and voices outside the mould of regular orchestrations. My aim was to bring these musics together in a fusion which would reflect both their essences and my own musical voice.'* Her first visit to Cape Town allowed her to jam with Amampondo, an internationally renowned traditional Xhosa percussion band from Langa Township. (Amampondo had developed a relationship with Valleys Kids in previous years and had inspired the vision of this bicultural project. They also formed part of the orchestra supporting this show.) Paula described that experience of playing with the band as unique, enabling her to

'They give what they can to strangers who already have so much.'

appreciate their different approach to time and pulse. That rhythm was then included in her symphony.

Against this combined artistic background many other levels of integration took place, within the South African groups, among the Welsh teams and between members of both countries. The different parties from Cape Town had not met each other before Mzansi Cymru. They had not even seen each other perform. Close friendships grew between the people from Africa on the visit to Cardiff in July, creating a wider support group for those with shared interests. Similarly, the group from the Welsh valleys had been quite separate until they travelled to Cape Town. ArtWorks and members of Mzansi Cymru choir and Extraordinary Ensemble stayed in the same hotel, participated in some activities together and learned more about each other, while enjoying each other's company.

Several of the Welsh contingent commented that it was not until they got to South Africa that they really understood why they were there and why they had taken part in such a venture. Visits to some of the townships brought home the degree of poverty that local people endured. A trip to Robben Island where Nelson Mandela, along with many others had been imprisoned for over 26 years spotlighted the painful struggle that they had undergone to help bring about an attitude of democracy in their home country. What impressed many of the visiting group was the quiet dignity of the residents of the townships and the exprisoners who had suffered for their political beliefs. Rachel from Artworks commented on the fact that the residents were grateful for everything they had. Dai was amazed too that they were so happy. *'They give what they can to strangers who already have so much.'* This group of young people believed we have much to learn about sense of community from the townships of South Africa.

'I love my blind friends but I want to be a normal person. The choir is where I feel most normal.'

What the Welsh group discovered very quickly on their trip to Cape Town was that although many inroads have brought greater choice for some, apartheid is not dead. They learned that few local white people visit these neighbourhoods preferring to live in their own bubble. Hannah discussed the contrast of visiting the townships and a walk through an area of downtown Cape Town where all the faces were black, with attending a performance of a philharmonic orchestra where the majority of the audience were predominantly white. Others noted the reaction of onlookers on the beach as they observed the Welsh youngsters picnicking and playing rugby together with some of the South African cast of Torchbearers. It was obvious that it was an unusual occurrence to see a mixed group in such close proximity and it produced a frisson of surprise among those who looked on. That ripple effect caused some of the observers to express their curiosity and then to decide that they wanted to attend the show, supporting the message of integration. Some of the ArtWorks team concluded that perhaps people could see more clearly what is happening in their own community through the eyes of strangers.

FULFILMENT OF NEED

'I love my blind friends but I want to be a normal person. The choir is where I feel most normal.'

Babs made this statement. She is totally blind and has other physical ailments that mean she has difficulty standing and walking. To get around, she has to use a wheelchair.

Along with her daughter Amy, Babs was one of the original members of the Welsh part of the Mzansi Cymru choir. For the 4 years of regularly attending rehearsals and shows,

Babs feels she has been part of a close-knit community. It is where she has found many friends and feels the most fulfilment. Other members gave her lifts so that she could attend rehearsals. Mother and daughter devised a special code so that she started each song in unison with others. In Cape Town, where the streets are not built to be wheelchair friendly, many of the members of the groups (young and not so young) volunteered to push her chair, taking some of the pressure off Amy and making sure that Babs attended every event. Babs was very clear in her belief that this support from others made it possible for her to take part in the whole process. Before the trip to South Africa, Amy and Babs performed in a concert, accompanied by friends, raising funds to help towards their expenses.

Amy (27) also found the experience of belonging to the choir personally fulfilling. It helped her decide what she wanted to do in life. With musical qualifications, she had not found her niche until then. Her obvious skills meant that she became one of the leaders in the choir, helping Paula with workshops. Gradually, she grew in confidence and learned to relax into her abilities. One of her most vivid experiences in South Africa was in taking part in a marimba and drum jamming session. The community leader in the township arts centre sang, moving and swaying to the rhythm, uninhibited in her enjoyment. *'That made up my mind for me. I decided I didn't care. I was going to take pleasure in the experience and express myself by moving to the music in choir practice, too.'* The regularly attended Mzansi Cymru choir continues with Amy as its leader. She is pursuing further training to help develop her skills in leading the musical chorus. Those that continue to come together to enjoy singing in the choir carry on the sense of community on a smaller scale.

Another member of the choir from Wales, Cariad Anne was 6 years old when she started attending with her mother, Claire. By the time they travelled to Cape Town to perform in the Artscape theatre, she was 10. Although they had not anticipated that they would travel that far, mother and daughter (who both love singing) decided that taking part in this project was something that they would do together. For the pair, the trip to South Africa was their first time abroad and first time flying on an aeroplane. Claire described the whole experience as *'amazing to go so far away and make new friends.'* Among many achievements, Cariad Anne talked of facing her fear of flying, climbing down the testing Table Mountain on foot, swimming in the Atlantic Ocean amid big waves and performing in Artscape. The visits to the townships have made them both more grateful for what they have in life.

SHARED EMOTIONAL CONNECTION

Connor from the ArtWorks team shared that he was glad that he had visited the townships on previous occasions. (Earlier, members of the ArtWorks team had visited some of the townships to make a film called In Somebody Else's Shoes.) It gave him the advantage *'of being able to support the others in dealing with the intensity of it all.'* He was sensitive to the fact that many of the facets of the Mzansi Cymru project touched participants deeply.

The emotional bonding between different individuals and groups was on many levels. One of those points of connection came from the collective pride in working toward and achieving an arts project of the highest standard. Another developed through gaining a better understanding of the difficult history and circumstances of 2 diverse communities. Visiting a country as non-tourists brings with it many deeper levels of knowledge and empathy.

Babs wrote a song about her powerful feelings that arose from her involvement in this project. She sang this to the rest of the community on the terrace of the hotel after one of the shows in Cape Town. I would like to borrow her eloquence of expression. Vividly, she describes her emotional connection:

TORCHBEARERS TRIBUTE

The 2012 Olympics mean so much to me
Though my back hurts too much to run and my eyes they just don't see
But I was part of something great that thrills me deep inside
Cultural Olympiad, you fill my heart with pride.

Chorus
So take me out to Africa. Lead me out to Africa.
I must go to Africa, Mzansi come with me.
From our valley mountains wide
Across the oceans deep divide
Take me out to Africa. I must go to Africa.
My heart it lies in Africa. I hear it calling me.

A play, a dream, a certainty there would come a day
When Valleys Kids would all unite with kids from far away.
South Africa and Wales would join in drama, dance and song
With Circus acts and acrobats and enthusiasm strong.

Would it really happen? Would it all come true?
With trials and tribulations, there was so much to do.

But Torchbearers, we held the flame of hope high in our hands:
The hope for change, the hope for peace and a world that understands.

We were all athletes on that day playing our small part
To achieve our goal, our miracle that lives within our hearts.
For as I stood there on the stage on the 20th of July
I felt so overwhelmed with pride and a tear was in my eye.

Barbara Protheroe.

Another undeniable emotional connection was formed at the final stage show at the Artscape Theatre in Cape Town. As with every performance that took place there, the house was full. The African audiences were even more positive in their response than their Welsh counterparts. In Cape Town, the finale of each of the 3 presentations was met with a full standing ovation. What was most special about the last night there was that the audience was made up of people from the townships. It was their painful story that had been borrowed for the purposes of this musical play and their warm accolade conveyed the level of their approval and support.

The sense of friendship, solidarity and community was recognised.

A LIFE-CHANGING EXPERIENCE

As I was interviewing a variety of members of the groups and probing about their involvement with Mzansi Cymru several people used the phrase *'It was a life-changing experience.'* This seemed to happen in different ways for

'It was a life-changing experience.'

different people.

For some it was about friendship: making friends with people with similar interests in the local vicinity as well as internationally. For others it was about raising their self-esteem by pushing the limits of a skill or talent. A few were enabled to see more clearly their goals in life and were supported by the group in aiming for them. Several enjoyed the experience of reaching outside their own boundaries and learning about another culture. A number of the young discovered that they were becoming more politically aware as a result of spending time in the African communities and facing issues of social injustice. Youngsters from both countries established that it was not only they who were having a tough time. Others of all age groups found they were challenging their own values. For the Welsh team, returning home from visiting the townships just before Christmas caused some to question their materialism. For many, it was a learning experience that a positive sense of community brings out the best in people, brings them closer, opens up all sorts of avenues and that it need not be confined to geographical areas.

For me, the phrase that encapsulates all of that learning, and brings about an understanding of that life-change is the wisdom of Ubuntu: *'I am who I am because of who we all are.'*

CHAPTER 12

The Challenge of Keeping Channels Open

'No voice, no choice. No choice, no voice.'

This rhyming couplet comes from the script of the aforementioned Torchbearers play written by Laurence Allan. In two brief lines it neatly summarizes the main message of this history of Valleys Kids.

When asking permission to quote these words I discovered they had originated from a rap song created by Kyle who was 16 at the time of its inception. Kyle has been a long time member of Valleys Kids youth clubs, a member of the Mzansi Cymru choir as well as a key participant of the Raptiles rap group whose rhythmic renditions have been well-viewed online. This phrase became an inspiration for a repeating theme of the effects of oppression throughout the musical. It is a reminder that an inability to speak out restricts our opportunities in life. On the other side of the coin, if life circumstances limit our options, voices are silenced: particularly those of the young growing up in marginalised neighbourhoods.

Following suit, I would like to keep the rhythm and message of this mantra going as I introduce the subject for this chapter and link its different approaches. I intend it to reverberate through the next few pages. It represents the constantly whispering reminder of social injustices that can be so easily ignored or denied. It explains the drive behind an organisation like Valleys Kids – which does listen and hears clearly. Also, it emphasises the commitment to listen by putting well-considered systems in place that simplify that process of hearing clearly. Much time, thought and energy has been devoted to creating methods that ease the flow of communication from the communities the charity serves.

The perpetual challenge for Valleys Kids and similar establishments is in finding ways to keep the channels of resources and communication open so that it can 'help others help themselves.' One of the very important messages of this book is the importance of relationship. I hope I have proved that this intense level of professional commitment is absolutely necessary for instigating interventions so that young people growing up in the South Wales valleys have more opportunities to express who they are and what they want. Thus having more chance to reach these goals despite the persistent social malaise of child poverty. The management of Valleys Kids strives to back up and maintain that necessarily high level of contact. It has put in place several frameworks that support that essential relationship: the importance of the primary worker who has face to face contact with the people the charity serves.

This final chapter covers some of the roles of the wider organisation of Valleys Kids. It focuses on how the charity functions and moves with the times; how it upholds its uniqueness and independence; how it continues to have its ears to the ground, listening to the voices of the community; how it searches for more and more ways to reach out to young people and their families to help them find ways to change their state of affairs; how it relates to other establishments with similar goals and how in the present economic climate it fights to provide new opportunities while hanging on to its core beliefs.

'Overcoming poverty is not a gesture of charity; it is an act of justice. It is a protection of a fundamental human right, the right to dignity and a decent life.'

Neslson Mandela

The challenge to keep open that intensity of communication with the community and to sustain that depth of intervention has not got easier over the years. The needs are still there. The hardship in these communities persists and the challenge to keep listening and to filter resources where they are most needed continues.

With the introductory chant playing in the background, I broach this subject of keeping open some of these channels of support under 3 different subtitles:

Channel A. **Asking for More** - the complexities of finding and maintaining financial pathways.

Channel B. **Standing Together** - the importance of working in partnership within and outside the organisation.

Channel C. **New Initiatives. The Factory** – a different route for Valleys Kids in helping empower local people to change their lives.

CHANNEL A - ASKING FOR MORE

'Overcoming poverty is not a gesture of charity; it is an act of justice. It is a protection of a fundamental human right, the right to dignity and a decent life.'

Nelson Mandela 2004

One of the main conduits that Valleys Kids does its utmost to keep flowing is through raising finances to support and maintain its staff, activities and buildings.

Historically in this area, miners donated 1 penny a week from their wages to the Miners' Welfare Fund. This central pool of money was altruistic in purpose and was often put towards recreational facilities like the building of miners' institutes. As well as providing areas for social interaction, they usually included a library to help with improving knowledge and education. The modern equivalent of the welfare fund is national insurance. The disadvantage of the present day system is that it is large, cumbersome and managed centrally, at a distance. The revenue does not find its way back in the required proportions to the impoverished communities that need most help.

Since the very beginning, the goal of Valleys Kids has been a commitment that no child or adult should be deprived of opportunities on financial grounds and that services should be free for all. As the preceding pages show, the charitable status of this organisation and the vision of the people working there, have given it an agility to reach out and engage with local communities that other organisations don't reach. Consequently, the relationships that are formed highlight the large pockets of continuing adversity in the South Wales valleys and make possible a creative response to a number of those needs. Obviously, this decision to deliver services free at the point of access calls for a long-term dedication to seeking out resources that enable young people and their families to reap many life-improving benefits.

One of the tasks of an organisation placed in the voluntary sector is to recognise the gaps in the community and find effective ways of filling them. Therefore, a major role of a charity such as Valleys Kids is to speak on behalf of the local families and ask for more money for this purpose. As the history of the organisation shows, Valleys Kids has been successful at negotiating funding and at responsibly meeting many of the needs of the area. With its main purpose of giving children and young people a better start in life, the additional capital is used to pay for different activities, to improve buildings and the environment and in so doing it encourages local people to reach for greater aspirations.

In the earlier days of Valleys Kids, there was a determination that projects would not be finance led. What this means is that rather than looking for a pocket of money and making a project fit into the donor's requirements, the organisation committed itself to finding out from the community what the needs were and then tried to find the funds to fulfil that request. The motive behind this plan was to encourage local people of all ages to believe they deserved more and that they had some say in the direction of the improvement of life in the valleys. Historically, Valleys Kids was very successful at acquiring funding and channelling it where the community required it most. At the time of initiation, those who supplied the sources of money were adaptable and prepared to follow the route planned by the organisation.

Today, it appears that it is more difficult to be as innovative and every stream of money comes with its complexities. In the present financial climate, Valleys Kids is still surviving and still able to find some sources of money but a lot of the flexibility to respond to need is being hampered. That is partly because of the lack of money, generally. Additionally, the dampening down of fresh ideas has happened as a result of the tightening of modern-day bureaucracy. Despite much literature encouraging the young people to be involved in decision making and to be heard on all matters which concern their lives, and although the Welsh Government appears to have had the best intentions in developing community involvement, financial structures have been created which dominate what goes on, on the ground. Listening to what local people say has taken less priority, it seems.

Richard Morgan, the funding director says, *'we used to have the freedom to do what we wanted to do. That is changing because of the deployment of tenders. Grants have been replaced by contracts. People who have the money have their own idea of what is needed. This limits the flexibility in responding to the community.'*

Denise Lord, whose task it is to coordinate the fund-raising for Valleys Kids finds a mixed response when appealing to the private sector. She sees her role as interpreting the needs of the communities in the Valleys (as the teams working there see them) to business people who may have their own perceptions of what is required. Many donors are enthusiastic in their response to the vision and energy of different Valleys Kids' projects and they are very generous and supportive in their comeback. However, some people living in different areas, who enjoy a more comfortable way of life, have little idea of the challenges that face the people of the valleys. Therefore, they have difficulty grasping what Valleys Kids is trying to do. Although invited, some business people are reluctant to come and see for themselves or to meet some of the service users.

Many benefactors have generously supported Valleys Kids in setting up and maintaining the projects over the years. Financial aid that has assisted the charity to help people restore their community in many ways comes from government, local authority, different charitable trusts and private donations.

BALANCING PRIORITIES

In England, what has become known as the Third
Sector has experienced difficulties in adjusting to the
bureaucratisation of the services that work with the young.
I quote from Work with Young People, a book published
in 2009 and written by a collection of contributors, all
experienced in the vast and varied field of working with
people in this age group. The following statement comes
from a chapter written by Tom Wylie on Youth Work and
the Voluntary Sector. Tom Wylie was Chief executive of the
National Youth Agency in England. He is now a trustee of
several national voluntary organisations. In his opinion:

*'Voluntary sector youth work has continued to diversify,
professionalise and flourish. It looks likely to remain a
favourite of politicians for the foreseeable future as it
gives the impression that at least some parts of it can
go further and faster (and perhaps more cheaply) than
those who are more direct servants of the state. But this
position of rhetorical advantage comes at a price. The
sector's increasing dependence on government funding
can challenge ways of working and values. It may also
bring with it approaches to managerial, administrative and
professional practice with which some of the sector will
be uncomfortable, and a challenge to independence of
thought and action.'*

While hanging on to its mission and independence, Valleys
Kids is aware that it must adapt in order to survive in
today's political and economic climate. The needs of the
young people in the South Wales valleys are still huge. If it
is to stay responsive to the requirements of the community,
it has to find new ways to raise money if it is to stay flexible
in its response to need. Also, if it is to continue to be an
advocate of involving the community in the decision-

making process, it must persist in negotiating ways of bridging the gap in communication between the corridors of power and the children and families it serves.

In the present financial circumstances, like everywhere else, Valleys Kids has to tighten its belt. To date, there has been a minimal loss of staff but everyone working there has not had a salary increment in several years. Until recently, it has been rare in Valleys Kids that money runs out for certain projects and unusual when crucial jobs are lost. However, redundancy does happen there too and as the recession was kicking in, the post of Community Advocate was lost, just as the need for free specialist advice on all kinds of problems arose. Lack of funding deleted a much-needed service to the community.

Perhaps the greatest effect of recent changes on staff and service users has been balancing the demands on time. The atmosphere of the charity has altered as it deals with the language and statistics of policy directives, performance indicators and targets. Also, how the organisation keeps its records has changed greatly in the last few years. Bureaucracy insists on huge amounts of paperwork which takes those trained to work within the community away from what they do best: building trusting relationships, coordinating different activities, being a professional friend and - having time to listen and help. If Valleys Kids is to stick to its values, then it has to ensure that the importance of skilled work with people is not eclipsed by the expectations of officialdom. Filtering the colourful and creative energy of young people through the greyness of management has its challenges.

Other organisations have a greater number of support staff. That is, more administration staff; more human resources personnel; more finance workers and more employees who know about computer systems. The management believes that if Valleys Kids were better off, it would be able to employ more people with these skills, which would help relieve the pressure on practitioners and management, as well as the skeleton support team.

There is evidence that Valleys Kids is learning to adjust in the way it raises income, in order to keep helping people in the area. Many of the present day funders will give money for helping people back into work; that is the major focus of this time. As a result, disadvantaged families are being helped in building confidence while preparing for entering or returning to the workplace. They have a say in what they would like to learn. The young benefit greatly from parents' improved self-esteem and from their own experience in this programme. The records and statistics are recorded diligently fulfilling the standards of both the funder and the organisation.

SOME STATISTICS

While making a case for the importance of maintaining a high level of communication and the need to search for continuing financial support, it is necessary to give some numbers to illustrate the size of the organisation's commitment.

In the year between 2011-2012 the total, membership of Valleys Kids was 2417. More than one half of that membership (57%) comes from Penygraig Community project. The rest were made up from Pen Dinas (111) Penyrenglyn (423) and Rhydyfelin (481). ArtWorks whose membership comes from the different areas in which Valleys Kids serves was 479. The age group served comes from the cradle to the grave and the greatest bulk of that membership is sourced from 0 to 16 year olds although all the older age groups are well represented too. Of that 2,417 – 1073 were male and 1377 were female. Please note that these statistics do not include the numbers of people attending shows and other community events that are also managed by the staff and volunteers, more often than not.

The amount of staff of Valleys Kids is usually around the 50 mark. About 40 of those are 'on the ground' coordinating the 4 centres, planning, managing and running different activities while training, supervising and working alongside over 100 volunteers in order to establish contact and relationships with members. The majority of staff are employed full time, about one fifth are part time. Although it can be rationalised that a lot of effective youth work and community work can be done in groups, the numbers above help to highlight the massive degree of listening required to keep doing the job effectively. It also illustrates the importance of the role of volunteers. All practitioners work unsocial hours in order to be available when young people need them most.

INSPIRING BUILDINGS

Valleys Kids' financial commitment is not only to keeping activities going. It has also taken some responsibility for raising the standard of the environment by creating attractive buildings. Although the surrounding countryside in Rhondda Cynon Taff is green and beautiful, the historic neighbourhoods running up the valleys have seen better days. The appearance of various areas is one of neglect as some buildings have been overlooked and abandoned for a while. The coal industry has left many scars on both the physical and socio-economic landscape.

*a sense of pride -
'this is where I come
from and it is worth
preserving.'*

As well as engaging directly with people living in the communities, Valleys Kids has been responsible for considerable improvement in the environment. It has upgraded significant buildings in the areas it serves, which has helped improve the morale of local people. Margaret Jervis (one of the founders and for some years now the Operational Director) has memories of how Valleys Kids started working in some unappealing buildings - like the now attractive, comfortable and very well used Penyrenglyn Project that was due for demolition. The organisation believed the people of the community deserved the best and the communities gradually changed in attitude as well as in looks, as everyone involved worked together to improve the fabric of each centre. This degree of participation brought a feeling of purpose, of belonging and a heightening of self-esteem. Another founder, Richard Morgan believes that the upgrading of buildings helps change the perception of the Valleys. It treats the past with respect, restoring a historic feeling of self (a sense of pride - *'this is where I come from and it is worth preserving.')*

Other chapters have covered the renovation of centres in Penygraig, Penyrenglyn, Pen Dinas and Little Bryn Gwyn and the fact that Rhydyfelin is looking for a more central base. (Later in the chapter we will discuss a new project – The Factory in Porth.)

Soar, the building that houses the Penygraig Community Centre is a state of the art theatre and facility catering for activities for all age groups in the locality. This has been the largest project of renovation that Valleys Kids has undertaken, so far. Situated on a conspicuous site at a roundabout on a through road, its attractive exterior is quite eye-catching. It lifts the mood of the surrounding community. The interior has brought many favourable comments, also. In order for the community to enjoy using the facilities, Valleys Kids raised 2.3 million pounds for the first phase of its renovation in 2005. The second phase of restoration occurred in 2006 when the organisation secured a further £700,000. This latter tranche of money was used to redesign the vestry of the original chapel into a community skills centre as well as an area in which the local congregation can meet.

Attractive buildings draw many people to meet at a central point, to participate in different activities, to try something new and to receive some support, if they want it. These centres of community also encourage an ease of contact and communication.

CHANNEL B - STANDING TOGETHER.

In order to be able to hear clearly the voices of the community, it takes a great deal of skill and dedicated teamwork to coordinate the professionals who act as a conduit, passing the necessary information on. This section considers some of the frameworks that have been put in place in order for organisations like Valleys Kids to reach out and support as many people as possible. It reviews both the internal structure of the organisation along with the links into a wider network of agencies.

During an interview with Margaret Jervis, I was reminded that 'Valleys Kids has always had a commitment to work in partnership with the local residents and with the agencies delivering services to the community.' Members of the local community (adults and young people) are also seen as partners of Valleys Kids. The early response of the community development project of *'We will help you if you help us'* established a pattern of united stances, of mutuality, of working through problems together.

Her husband, Richard Morgan, the Funding Director, affirms that the voluntary organisation tries to follow a modern interpretation of the value of the former mining communities where each person tried to support the other. They both assert the belief that *'we have to work together – no one organisation can tackle the enormity of the challenge alone.'*

Joined-up thinking is integral to how Valleys Kids operates. It is how it keeps its channels of communication open and how the organisation shows that it wants and respects the input of the young and adult service users. Over the years, that spirit of cooperation has been nurtured within the network of staff and volunteers. It also applies between the community centres and the children and families they serve. There are formal as well as informal methods of gathering opinions from local residents. Major ventures like the improvement of Little Bryn Gwyn have required consultations with all age groups in all Valleys Kids' areas. The renovation of Soar Centre in Penygraig came after much consultation with the local community.

Professionals from a variety of disciplines influenced the journey of Valleys Kids. In the earlier years of the project, probation officers, social workers, teachers and youth workers all pooled resources and worked together in the same building for the benefit of the young of the area. There are many recounted memories from the pioneers of this organisation of long and heated debates. Through that mutual support and creative discussion many innovative approaches evolved. Most of those are described in previous chapters.

Penygraig Community Project expanded into Valleys Kids partly through a pathway provided by the development of outreach play schemes. This impetus was instigated by the teamwork of several organisations including social services and the community development staff of the project. Health workers have also contributed greatly to the fruition of this charity that rose to meet the needs of the local population.

Julie Spiller gives her account of the early days of the Penyrenglyn Project and the many inter-agency discussions that led to its development. She saw an added bonus in working with her partners. Initially, many professionals came together with the common aim of improving the health of mothers and babies. A number of those colleagues faced tough and challenging jobs. In meeting collectively to explore ways of helping families, they discovered that they had formed a professional support group that helped them as individuals. As they backed one another and bounced ideas off each other, they built self-confidence, stimulating new thought processes, and finding new ways to respond to the community. Not only did the people in the neighbourhood benefit, the professionals did too.

MINDING THE GAPS

In the present day, the networks that link Valleys Kids to other institutions within the community are large and diverse. The three members of the management team along with some other members of staff are committed to partnership work. Margaret devotes some of her time to supporting other agencies. Her dedication to Play Wales, at a national level, is vast. She also sits on the boards of the Arts Council for Wales and Wales Council for Voluntary Action (WCVA). Pauline is active in her support of the development of Communities First and plays a major role as a voluntary sector representative in Canopi, a framework for better integrating of services to children and young people. As director of the organisation's funding programme, Richard has committees that he supports too. The coordinators of the local projects are involved with others in the local Communities Regeneration projects. The ArtWorks team has several partners in the Arts world and Mzansi Cymru has taken partnership to a global level having partners in South Africa, as well as in this country.

The Way Ahead, the strategic plan of 2013- 2016 states that *'Valleys Kids has always argued the importance of working in partnership if we are going to support and empower people and communities.'* Margaret Jervis emphasises that the organisation is committed to working in partnership with statutory agencies, including Rhondda Cynon Taf Children's Services and other voluntary organisations to support children and young people to find solutions to their needs. Indeed, the charity has been instrumental in helping to set up different committees and projects with the purpose of combining skills and resources. This is particularly true in the development of play opportunities. Valleys Kids were founder members of Play Wales, the All Wales Play Forum, Rhondda Play Project, Rhondda Play Forum and the Rhondda Cynon Taf Play Association.

One of the most recent partnerships, in which Valleys Kids is involved, resulted in the development of the Confident Kids: Confident Families programme described in Chapter 9. Through consultation with local people and organisations, it established that there was a gap in service in the community when it came to supplying confidence-building support for families of 5 to 11 year olds. The formation of Canopi highlighted this need. Canopi is part of Rhondda Cynon Taf's Children and Young People's Partnership. This multi-agency approach provides a framework, which promotes the following aims, ensuring:

- *'Better access to services for children, young people and their families;*
- *More integrated delivery of services, and*
- *Better matching of services to local and individual needs.'*

Placed in the heart of the locality, Penygraig Community Project provides the hub for this integrated service delivery in Mid Rhondda. Canopi is in the process of being rolled out into other parts of the community.

New projects have arisen for the Family Training Team through working in close partnership with others. As the governmental benefits system changed, they found they could no longer work with those on Job Seeker's Allowance. So they liaised with other agencies such as Children's Services, Women's Aid, Sure Start and Flying Start listening for the areas of need where they could best bring their specialist skills. As a result, they are now working with more vulnerable parents with complex needs. These families may be suffering from problems such as domestic abuse, drug and alcohol issues or mental health problems. The children concerned are on the Children in Need register or under Child Protection.

Running alongside this, the team has also been involved in another initiative called Team Around the Family (TAF). This is part of the All Wales Intervention, which aims to work with families at earlier stages. That is families with emerging needs where the children have not been placed on the aforementioned registers. This project arose for Valleys Kids out of a gap in the community where agencies wanted to refer family members to parenting groups but found there were none in the particular area. Consequently, the Family Training Team was able to bring its expertise, helping to facilitate intervention before a crisis escalated.

A PARTNERSHIP WITHIN

As Valleys Kids grew, much thought went into creating an internal organisational structure that would best facilitate the flow of communication from the young people and their families. Early planning started with the ideal of encouraging the community to run and take responsibility for the projects themselves. However, the laws of governance put restrictions on those values. Therefore, the organisation has strived to keep the formation of the hierarchy as flat as possible to enable the community to have a major say in how Valleys Kids help fulfil their needs.

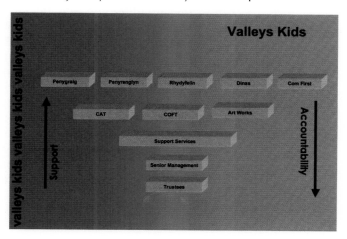

The framework of the organisation is designed and portrayed as an inverted triangle with the community at the top. The flow of support percolates upward towards the different communities and the staff that serve them. (At the same time the channel of accountability filters down through the structure of the organisational diagram.) The network of support tapers from the community centre staff members who are backed by the itinerant teams of

Community Access to Technology, The Family Training Team and Artworks. In turn, they are upheld by the Support Services and Senior Management, followed by the trustees of the organisation who are placed in to the base position. The structure is intended as an easy conduit of information throughout the establishment. It is planned this way so that all levels of the organisation can hear clearly and pass on information on what local young people and their families require.

In this book, much emphasis has been put on the grassroots workers but behind the scenes other members of staff play an important role. Backing the organisation, assisting and managing the teams who are working 'with an ear to the ground' is another group of Valleys Kids employees. In the headquarters of the organisation at Cross Street, Penygraig, there is a small team of Support Workers, as well as Margaret, Richard and Pauline who make up the Senior Management Team. The support team consists of 2 administration staff, 2 fundraisers and 2 people dealing with the finance. Different volunteers also help in the admin office. They all play a significant and crucial role in supporting the work of the practitioners as well as the managers. Bringing their skills to the wider picture, they are an essential part of the team.

Members of the administrative staff are seen as lynchpins of the organisation. As the people who answer the telephone and greet everyone who walk in the door (visitors, members of the community and staff), they provide the frontline point of contact. They are the gatherers of information from the different teams in the organisation. They record the data given for evaluation projects. They keep statistics up to date for managers, for potential funders as well as the trustees of Valleys Kids. At the same time, local people come in and ask them for practical help with various issues. For example, at this crucial time of mounting unemployment, they have been faxing off information to employers for local people looking for work. Placed in reception, by the front door, they often find themselves in the role of 'calmers down', helping out when different colleagues deal with the mounting demands of their work.

Two people make up the finance team and deal with the accounts of the organisation. I met with one of the pair who also saw her role as supporting other members of staff 'so they can concentrate on what they do for the community.' She sees her job as not just paying bills or writing cheques. She recognises that staff struggle with huge amounts of paperwork. So, the finance team deal with purchase orders finding the best place to get what is needed, seeking the best deal and negotiating on behalf of the charity.

Along with the directors, the fundraising team has a huge challenge in raising enough funds so that the organisation can continue to be flexible and innovative in its response to the huge needs of the community. It is also taxed with the responsibility of finding funding to keep pilot schemes going after the original source of money runs out.

OVERSEEING AND UNDERPINNING

Overseen by coordinators at a team level, the overall responsibility of supervising and supporting the dedication and passions of the *'people on the ground'* come under the remit of the Senior Management Team. It is at this level that there is a prioritising of what community needs may be met and a consideration of how funds can be raised to meet some of those requests. The two-way funnelling of communication occurs in the Staff Core Team that is made up of coordinators of the different work groups, along with the managers of the organisation.

There are 3 people in the Management Team of Valleys Kids where executive decisions are made. They are Margaret Jervis, Operational Director, Richard Morgan, Funding Director and Pauline Richards, Community Development Manager. Richard is responsible for managing all the financial demands of the organisation, making sure that all systems are secure and that detailed accounts are available to be checked through when required. Margaret is support manager to several of the coordinators of the different projects. Also, a major part of her role is to deal with the legalities and practice required for Human Resources. Pauline also supports several coordinators of teams. She synchronizes the Valleys Kids training programme and keeps staff communication open about the use of Little Bryn Gwyn. All three are committed to building partnerships with other organisations in the county, as well as nationwide.

The people who put themselves at the bottom of the triangle but actually have the legal responsibility of governance for Valleys Kids are the Board of Trustees. They have the overall planning viewpoint of the organisation. Different documents, including the original business plan for The Factory, describe their role as the following: *'The Board is responsible for the overall governance of the organisation including setting strategic direction and agreeing the financial plan. The Board acts on advice and information from regular meetings with the senior managers. Decisions made at other levels of the organisation are reported to the board.'* Although the trustees set the strategic direction, the initial ideas for the business plan come from within the Community Projects and the other specialist areas of work. This information is coordinated by and channelled through the executive directors of Valleys Kids to the Board.

The Board of Trustees is accountable for ensuring that the organisation is well run. It has a right to challenge the staff and management on why they are making certain decisions. Fulfilling a more distant and independent perspective, these members of the board voluntarily accept this role because they have a long-term commitment to the organisation. The chairman, Dr Howell Edwards was the original founder member of what was to become Valleys Kids over 30 years ago. With many years of service in Probation and subsequently in managing all aspects of Children's Services, he has been chairman since Valleys Kids inception. There are 7 members of the board who bring their knowledge of social services, probation, health, social enterprise and local communities.

In recent times, one of the new enterprises brought to the Board for their approval comes in the form of The Factory.

CHANNEL C – NEW INITIATIVES.

Internationally, the Rhondda Valleys were regarded as having shaped an industrial powerhouse during the coal-mining era. Sadly, since the closure of the pits those days have gone and little has been created to replace those very important livelihoods. There remains a huge void of meaningful employment in this area.

In the present day, what Valleys Kids hears very clearly is that some of this area's greatest assets are in the young – in their energy, their creativity, their curiosity and their enthusiasm for life. Generally, this huge potential has been undervalued and often discouraged. Unless more

is done to support, encourage and develop that promise much is going to be lost. At best, the more courageous will leave the valleys and explore pastures new. At worst, that precious energy will be repressed or denied and many talented people will end up enduring long-term unemployment or just surviving in dead end jobs.

Over the years, Valleys Kids has heard that call for help and responded in different ways. More recently, it has been exploring new and innovative avenues to help young people follow their hopes and dreams (along with the not so young). It is hoped that many can find a positive future in the growing cultural industries of South Wales, which may enable more to stay in their home area and not migrate to pastures new.

THE FACTORY

While The Factory is a different venture for the organisation, it meets many of the criteria mentioned in this chapter.

- It brings to life an iconic historical building in Porth, the gateway of the Rhondda valleys.
- It provides new and potential sources of income for the charity - this time through social enterprise and a new business arm of Valleys Kids.
- Through the creative arts, it helps people raise their expectations by encouraging them to develop new creative skills that will make it possible for them forge a career in the established cultural industries of South Wales.

Formerly known as the Pop Factory, the building has a history of bottling Corona Lemonade, a carbonated drink that was popular throughout the United Kingdom.

A beacon on the Porth skyline for over 100 years, built on the bend of the river and with an imposing tower, it is seen from most parts of the surrounding community. Many of the original features remain in the building.

Providing employment for generations of valleys' people over the years, it has produced a variety of materials and in the year 2000 was changed into an award winning television production studio that enjoyed an international reputation. With the vision of transforming it further into a hub for the cultural industries, Valleys Kids had the opportunity to purchase the building in 2010. A document called The Pop Factory: Creative Space for the Valleys asserts – *'Through saving an iconic building and developing it as a cultural enterprise, we aim to communicate the message to local people, and to the wider Wales, that the valleys have had a great past but they also have a great future.'*

SOCIAL ENTERPRISE

Still surviving strongly in the precarious atmosphere of financial recession, Valleys Kids' aim is to develop as varied a funding portfolio as possible. While its core income comes from Local Authority and the Welsh Government, generous strands of money from charitable trusts, corporate sponsors and individual donations have also supported its work. Through The Factory and the new business arm of Valleys Kids (called Valleys Creative), the intention is to find some autonomy by raising self-generated income. Much of this is to be achieved through Social Enterprise.

Generally, there appears to be much confusion about what this phrase means. According to a book named The Art of Social Enterprise written by Frankel and Bromberger, such a business is defined as: *'…an organisation formed by one*

or more people whose commercial activities are primarily driven by the desire to create economically sustainable positive change.' Elise Stewart, the Project Coordinator of The Factory, clarifies this further: *'The term Social Enterprise means that Valleys Creative is a trading company that makes a profit for social good. The income The Factory raises goes back into social development.'* Therefore, the commitment of Valleys Creative is that the rewards of the business will be used to help support the development of Valleys Kids' projects. Consequently, this means that more young people will be helped to find ways to raise their aspirations and to find a route into purposeful employment.

At this time, The Factory is evolving and is best known for its association with music. While the site lends itself to live musical performances, a challenge in this economic climate is to discover how to best to keep the momentum going, thus raising significant funds from them. John Davies, the Venue Coordinator has been tasked with developing that particular arm of The Factory as a location for such shows. His role is to explore what audiences and performers can be attracted to Porth. Among his many achievements, Rhondda Rocks (a 3 day music concert) is returning to The Factory in August 2013 to celebrate the musical abilities of this genre in South Wales.

Already established as a performance venue, The Factory also houses several creative and cultural industries including a film production company, graphic designers and sound engineers. The building is available for private hire for weddings and conferences, while the basement is rented out as a storage space to a local theatre group. Along with the revenue collected at the bar, these creative projects already provide a source of income for the company, which in turn will benefit others.

THE NURTURING OF CREATIVE ABILITIES

Undeservedly, so many people find themselves stuck in a rut. Those who are attracted to The Factory come because they are unemployed and looking for different job prospects. Others feel a pull towards that venture because they are in a dead-end job where they cannot demonstrate their creativity. Some of the young have been crushed in early employment and dismissed as no good. Those who work at The Factory believe that if you put the majority of these men and women in a different environment and give them the right opportunities and support - they shine.

That is what The Factory provides – a different environment. The culture there reaches for several goals. Among them are the following:

- To provide job club services that give support to individuals who are unemployed or who are already employed but have greater aspirations. This may include inviting speakers who have set up their own businesses and would like to share their own learning curve with others.
- To target those who have been let down by or who have failed in the education system. The factory provides a different method, which many find more comfortable and appropriate to them. Training courses are provided for all levels of interest up to university standard.
- To provide a safe place which encourages mutual respect where people can consider and progress their individual form of art in a relaxed atmosphere. The ambience encourages individuals from several parts of the Rhondda valleys to mix with people from different neighbourhoods with similar interests. This generates an informal support group system.

'I have been looking all my life for a place where you can get job satisfaction.'

- Voluntary Work is an essential part of the Factory as it is in other parts of Valleys Kids. At the time of writing this, several people are being recruited for training as stage managers for the Rhondda Rocks festival and as curators for the art exhibitions. Both the training and the subsequent voluntary work may well provide another *'string to ones bow'* and will look good on a growing curriculum vitae. The voluntary work is done on a time banking system which means that for every 2 hours accrued, the volunteer will gain points which earns them free tickets to artistic events or learning activities.

The ArtsWork department of Valleys Kids is based in The Factory, as is the 'Artist in Residence'. As described in previous chapters ArtsWork does much work to introduce children and young people to the Arts and to explore and develop their creativity from an early age.

Some of the responsibilities of Anne Evans, the Artist in Residence include taking painting classes out into the communities and developing the top floor of the building as an important exhibition space for local artists. Already, this very attractive space has drawn several creative people wanting to exhibit their work.

In The Factory, the encouragement is for people of all ages to look into their potential and to discover where it takes them.

BRINGING OUT THE BEST IN PEOPLE.

Martin is in his 50s and had been unemployed for over 30 months before he became involved with The Factory. As well as coping with the stress of that, he has recently gone through a divorce. He describes himself as ' *being at a low ebb'* when he first met Elise. Martin's multiple past work experiences that included running his own business had done little to fulfil him. *'I had been used to working in a big factory where I am just a name and a number. I have been looking all my life for a place where you can get job satisfaction.'*

During his 10 months placement at The Factory, Martin has been working towards an ITEC qualification in administration. Among other tasks, his hands-on involvement means that he has been very involved with developing the organisational side of the enterprise. He has helped streamline systems and assists the businesses that rent a space by aiding them to integrate into wider venture. In turn, he learns from their creative experience. Additionally, he coordinates Health and Safety and is the first point of contact for visitors to the project.

I borrowed the phrase about *'bringing out the best in people'* from him. It describes what he feels has happened to him since he had a training placement at The Factory. He has also witnessed other participants benefiting from the same confidence-building process. Martin likes being part of a big family or team. He says that he is excited to be part of the enterprise and now he can't imagine working anywhere else.

With the help of The Factory, Sam is another person who has managed to start the reversal of that downward spiral of rejection and dejection. He is 27 years old and has a diploma in Art and Design. Recognising that he required further artistic qualifications if he wanted to pursue his dreams, he eventually applied to several colleges of art to be turned away by them all. As a result he became despondent, suffered panic attacks and slid further into depression. He rarely left the house, except to go across the road to the shops. His mother (who had become very worried about his isolation and lack of motivation) contacted Anne from The Factory. By degrees, he engaged with the art group there and gained more confidence in his abilities. He is aware that slow, gentle pressure is being put on him *'to make something'* of himself but he appreciates it is at a pace that he can cope with, at this time. Through The Factory he has completed different courses - one in First Aid, another in filmmaking. Each time he tries something different his confidence expands.

I asked Sam how he measured his growing self-confidence. His immediate reply was: *'If you had asked to meet with me a year ago I don't think there would have been a hope in hell of me talking to you!'* He wanted to do that now because he felt he had benefited from his involvement in the project and he wanted to pass that experience on. He went on to say that he has had to go to a number of medical boards recently to assess his availability for work. He is now able to attend on his own. Previously, he would have needed his mother at his side. He is also quite proud that he has managed to stop smoking, which he puts down to the positive influence of The Factory.

Recently, Sam has undergone some operations on nerves in his arms and he may need more on his legs. It will take time for him to heal but he is not despondent. Gradually, he is gaining faith in his abilities. Steadily, he is working towards his vision of working in the Arts. Realistically, he is lowering his expectations so he puts less pressure on himself while still aiming to fulfil his creative yen.

Both of the men mentioned here described the benefits of being listened to. Both appreciated the *'personal touch'* from the staff at The Factory. Both valued and acknowledged that what was heard very clearly - was what they were *'good at'*. Both welcomed the guidance of being given the appropriate training that starts them on a path to achieving what they are really capable of and really interested in.

VOICES AND CHOICES

In the closing of this final chapter of the book, it is important to return to it's beginning and to reflect on the mantra: *'No voice, no choice. No choice, no voice.'*

All of the people I have interviewed (about 200) have said in many different ways that is what Valleys Kids does well. It listens and hears what the communities are saying. It responds imaginatively to the challenge of that chant. It facilitates options in life by helping to raise expectations and having *'a can do attitude'*. It does that through the professional befriending, dedication and work of the staff and volunteers *'on the ground.'* It also achieves all of its goals through the clear vision, well planned strategies, accessible channels of communication and steady back up of the founders, management team, support staff and trustees. In Valleys Kids all of these criteria and dedicated people are interdependent on each other. They combine to make their own powerfully creative force. They have come together to make a difference in the lives of so many young people, along with their families and their communities.

In short, Valleys Kids encourages individual and collective voices to speak out and responds by helping a person or group of persons to find different choices in their lives. In so doing, it helps raise many horizons.

CONCLUSION

Message for the Future

'What happened in our past
Contributes to the present
And what happens in the present
Defines our future.'

This excerpt did not come from the South Wales valleys. It came from Nottingham and is attributed to Teean Smith-Robinson. As well as being Miss Black Britain 2009, Teean is a young freelance playwright and producer. In October 2009, she produced a play featuring young black people from across Nottingham entitled Re-rooted. It was part of a festival celebrating black history and culture.

What her innovative project has in common with Valleys Kids is the recognition of the abilities and talents of young people (including many of those from deprived backgrounds) and the skills of the staff, who find ways to help develop those aptitudes. Although the stories of the different groups of young people are quite diverse, the acquired quotation describes quite accurately the position of young people in Rhondda Cynon Taf, in the present time. The history of the closure of the mines has a huge impact on the lives of youngsters of today, still. How they are treated by society in the present will have huge repercussions for tomorrow.

Poverty, in whatever form it comes, has a way of marginalising people. Present day civilization, whether in England or Wales is not proving to be very successful in reducing the numbers of children living in dire circumstances. Nor is it doing enough to improve the dearth of employment for our young people. There are still many lessons to be learned about how best to approach and deal with the injustice of inequality. Much of that understanding must be concerned with the releasing of so much latent potential that has been repressed, particularly in our young.

Valleys Kids' experience of over 30 years is one way of engaging and working with communities that have suffered from devastating political decisions, of helping them change lives for the better. So, what does the history of the organisation show us? What of the young people? What have they told us about their experience of living in the valleys today? What do they have to teach us? What does their future hold for them? How have the pages of this book educated us about giving children the strongest roots and the most powerful wings in order to get the best out of life; as well as putting the most into it?

In doing the research for this study I was given a humbling learning experience. I almost missed one of the main messages that different individuals were telling me because a prejudice was blocking my hearing. I admit, I can be quite intolerant of what I think is society's over-preoccupation with safety. While I do not want youngsters to come to any harm, I worry that too much protectiveness can restrict them and can hold them down. So when a number of young people told me that what Valleys Kids did for them was help them feel safe, I was somewhat dismissive of that point, at first. However, that theme kept popping up. Kids in all age groups and from different areas repeated that message over and over again. Family members echoed the same appreciation. So, I started to be more attentive and enquired about what they meant when they talked of *'feeling safe'*. I began to listen properly and heard what they wanted to tell me.

What I learned was that young people value safety in quite a different way from adults. Health and safety was not the issue here. In fact, their behaviour showed that in spite of many adults' over-protectiveness, they were prepared to take risks, they wished to push the boundaries, and they had the urge to experiment with what they could do. They yearned to stretch themselves and have new experiences and they hankered to discover their fullest capabilities. What they were describing was the feeling of being included and of belonging. Valleys Kids gave them that security and that was what they valued.

What was conveyed to me was that Valleys Kids makes it easier for young people to feel safe because it accepts who they are. The relationships they have formed there help them believe that the organisation is on their side. Many appreciated that Valleys Kids believed in their promise. Knowing that there were expectations about certain behaviours, part of the feeling of security came from being contained and yet having the space to expand. Within that environment they were able to try different activities and discover the size of their capacities.

It is necessary to repeat that the young people mentioned in this book have grown up in an area whose foundations were rocked in years gone by and that recovery of these communities is a very slow process. Uncertainty about the future is their inheritance. That old feeling of insecurity is amplified in the present day. This intensification comes from living in an atmosphere where there are still high levels of child poverty; where there are low expectations; where many are in trouble with alcohol and drugs; where there is a high rate of suicide of young people and where there is one of the highest degrees of teenage pregnancy in Europe. Among others, all these worrying factors combine and together they contribute to young peoples' feeling of vulnerability. According to one source, in England and Wales more than 1 in 5 young people feel they have no future due to the recession. It is a struggle to build up hope in the present economic atmosphere. Indeed, it has taken great effort for decades.

So, exactly what is it that Valleys Kids gives to them? How does it intervene in the continuing poor conditions in the neighbourhood that it serves? How has it contributed to rebuilding the community?

For many, their particular observation of Valleys Kids centre was as a sanctuary, a place where they met friends, 'hung out,' tried different activities and had fun. Some attended regularly to escape the tensions at home; several came to be reassured when they constantly hit a brick wall when trying to find a job; while others preferred the more informal attitude of the community centre to the pressures of school, where they perceived that only the high achievers received adequate attention. In this environment, one or two felt protected from themselves, finding that habitual attendance of the youth club kept them off the streets and out of trouble.

In meeting with volunteers and other young people to discuss why Valleys Kids is such a mainstay in their lives, one of the first answers I was given was that it was local. The centres are close at hand, making it easier to meet with friends. Having a *'tidy'* place to go was important. (*'It makes me feel tidy'* was said quite often when describing the building involved and the ambience created there). Another perceived advantage was that many of the staff

**Valleys Kids has
become part of the
framework of the
neighbourhoods it
serves.**

grew up in the valleys and lived locally. There was a
common history, an understanding of circumstance.
Additionally, seeing the older members develop skills, train
professionally and take a responsible job in the community
inspired many of the young to want what they had
achieved and to believe success was possible for them too.

Longevity was also crucial to Valleys Kids' popularity
and stability. The organisation has been around for a
long time. At least 2 generations (and in some families
3) have participated in Valleys Kids' activities. Long-term
relationships have been established, creating a sense of
trust. In communities where fear of professionals and
bureaucracy is definitely an issue, that endurance of the
organisation earns many points. Valleys Kids has become
part of the framework of the neighbourhoods it serves.
Important to many residents, it is seen to be separate
from the statutory organisations like Education, Children's
Services, Police and Job Centres. It fulfils a role, providing
a place of easy access where families can drop in and
receive support.

The older teenagers with whom I met in all 4 centres
appreciated being treated like an equal. This attitude of
parity manifested itself in being trusted to make decisions
about the project, being given responsibility to help others
and an overall awareness that people from all backgrounds
were treated the same. Interestingly, most of the young
people did not feel that equality happened in other areas of
their lives.

The sense of 'family' was mentioned over and over again
as contributing to that overall sense of security. Some were
glad that their own close relatives had received support,
too. Many were very grateful for the intimacy of their club
and the time that was spent helping individuals sort out

personal problems and difficulties in relationships. (*'We can talk about anything here.'*) All who spoke to me were aware that the organisation had their best interests at heart and wanted the greatest prospects for their futures.

Several were mindful that involvement with Valleys Kids had opened all sorts of opportunities through play, the arts, new experiences, different activities, volunteer work and day-to-day encouragement. The wide base of interest of staff and volunteers opened many doors for them. Some had found career paths through that participation; many discovered what they were capable of and the majority of those with whom I spoke could see the increase in their self-belief and their ambition.

The above paragraphs bring together the responses to the first 2 questions of the research mentioned in the introduction. These were:

1 Why is this group/club/organisation important to you?
2 What has it done to help you?

The majority of those with whom I met were very vocal in their answers to these enquiries. The comeback to the third question of what would make Valleys Kids better was more hesitant. A few looked blank. The majority said that the organisation was fine as it was. Thirty-one young people and sixteen adults suggested more trips away from home. Little Bryn Gwyn was high on that agenda.

Valleys Kids stretches itself to its fullest capacity to keep filling that gap in the valleys' social structure: aiding young people to find the skills to help themselves to a positive future. The organisation struggles sometimes because the powers-that-be do not always understand the flexibility it needs to respond to what it hears from the communities it serves and do not always appreciate the importance of its role of intervention. However, that is part of its job – establishing itself in the heart of the neighbourhood, passing on the needs of the area to the relevant people, encouraging members of that community to speak up and ask for what they deserve; acting as an intermediary, making sure that local people are heard.

THE GIFT OF LISTENING PROPERLY

'I know that you believe you understand what you think I said, but I am not sure you realize that what you heard is not what I meant!'

Above all, the youngsters who were interviewed for this book felt appreciated in the atmosphere of Valleys Kids because they believe they were listened to at a local level and heard. Organisations that place themselves in the centre of the community with their ear to the ground are greatly needed because not everyone has acquired the skill to do that. Listening properly demands giving time to hear what is being said. It requires an engagement, a relationship, a respect and a commitment. If we do not communicate thoroughly with people we leave them perplexed and confused as the quotation above suggests. The quip, which is believed to have come from American politician, Senator Robert McCloskey, sums up many difficulties in hearing correctly.

Increasingly, Valleys Kids role is to ensure that people in power are really hearing what the communities are saying. Generally, human beings have lost the skill of listening. In our busyness, we presuppose what others are telling us. We mishear or misinterpret. We don't check out our

assumptions. Sometimes, we fill in the gaps wrongly. As a result, we miss the most important information and act accordingly. Often unwittingly, we step on people who do not find it easy to raise their voice.

In today's political climate, we tend to fall back on the statistics of outcomes studies to convince ourselves that we can hear the needs of communities and to prove whether the projects that are put in place work – or not. Sadly, data of this kind shows only part of the story. Relying on forms does not touch the circumstances in which people live. Nor does paperwork acknowledge the reality of the human stories, or witness how lives are changing.

I hope that this book goes some way to proving that society misses out on so much in ignoring or repressing that vibrant energy of children and young people. What many of these youngsters have shown me is that with the support of a community development organisation like Valleys Kids, they find the budding abilities to be leaders in their communities, to be creative in music and the arts or to develop business skills. Many also discover the ability to engage with other people and reach out to help them. That entire range of rich potential is wasted if we do not hear them properly. Given the right opportunities, the future will benefit greatly from the input of children and young people today.

However, what of the many other areas that do not have an organisation like Valleys Kids at its centre? How are they heard?

It is absolutely essential that this book does not pass over the main message that the young people of Rhondda Cynon Taf are relaying through Valleys Kids. It needs to be shouted from the rooftops until people hear it clearly and appreciate it as a gift for the present as well as the future. The message is:

'Give us a chance! We have a lot to give! Our potential is huge!!'

I wonder. Can you really hear them?

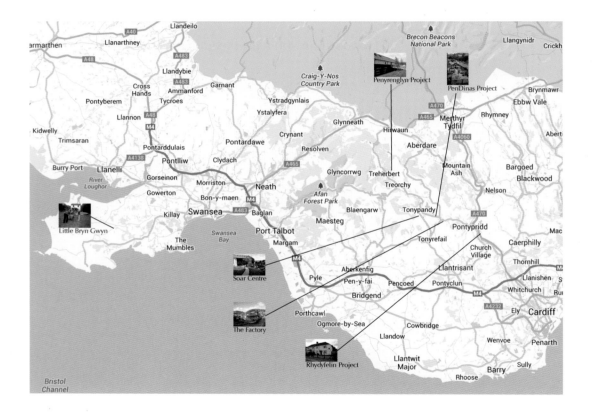

Llandeilo

A40

armarthen   Llanarthney

A48

Cross Hands   Llandybie
A483
Llanarthney   Garnant   Ammanford
Tycroes

Pontyberem   A48
Kidwelly   Llannon   A48
Trimsaran   M4
Pontarddulais
Burry Port   A4138
Llanelli   Pontlliw   Clydach
River Loughor   Gorseinon   Morriston
Gowerton   Bon-y-maen
Killay   Swansea   A483   Baglan
The Mumbles   Swansea Bay   Port Talbot
Margam

Craig-Y-Nos Country Park

Ystradgynlais
Ystalyfera
Crynant
Pontardawe   Resolven
A465
Glynneath
Glyncorrwg
Afan Forest Park
Blaengarw
Maesteg
M4
Pyle   Aberkenfig
Pen-y-fai
Bridgend
Porthcawl
Ogmore-by-Sea

Brecon Beacons National Park

Llangynidr   Crickh

Penyrenglyn Project   PenDinas Project   Brynmawr
Ebbw Vale

Hirwaun   Merthyr Tydfil   Rhymney   A470
A465   A4060   Abert
Aberdare
Mountain Ash   Bargoed   Blackwood
Treherbert   Nelson
Treorchy
Tonypandy   A470
Pontypridd   Mac
Tonyrefail   Church Village   Caerphilly
Llantrisant   Thornhill   M
Pencoed   Pontyclun   Llanishen   S
A4232   M4   Whitchurch   Ru
Llandow   Cowbridge   Ely   Cardiff
Llantwit Major   Wenvoe   Penarth
Rhoose   Barry   Sully

Little Bryn Gwyn

Soar Centre

The Factory

Rhydyfelin Project

Bristol Channel

REFERENCES

CHAPTER 1 – VOICES FROM THE PAST

Adamson Dave and Stephens Meic. Living on the Edge – Changing Wales.

Beckman Books Inc (1996).

BBC Primary History. Children in Victorian Britain. BBC.

Easton Mark Mark Easton's UK. BBC (2009).

Francis Hywel. History on Our Side. Wales and the 1984-85 Miners' Strike. Iconau (2009).

Freese Barbara. Coal – A Human History. Arrow Books (2006).

Save the Children Annual Report UK 2005 published (2006).

Save the Children Annual Report UK 2011 published (2012).

Tomkinson, Roy. Of Boys, Men and Mountains. Y Lolfa Cyf. (2005).

Welsh Coalmines. www.welshcoalmines.co.uk/GlamEast/DinasRhondda/htm.

Report from Valleys Kids archives: Valleys Kids. Hidden Potential. (1996).

CHAPTER 2 – FINDING ANSWERS

Wilkinson Richard and Pickett Kate The Spirit Level - Why Equality is Better for Everyone. Penguin Books (2010).

Reports from Valleys Kids archives:

Annual Report of Penygraig Community Project (1978/79)

H.M. Inspectors report on Penygraig Community Project. (1989). Welsh Office.

Working Together – Penygraig Community Project (1991)

Action Plan for Penygraig Community Project (1993/94)

Mission Statement Valleys Kids

CHAPTER 3 – LISTENING TO THE PENYRENGLYN COMMUNITY PROJECT

Perry Christian and the people of the Penyrenglyn project. Not Ready for Drowning –video Valleys Kids (2000).

Reports from Valleys Kids archives:

Forward Together Development Plan. Penygraig Community Project
Penyrenglyn Community Profile. Bridges Community Support Team
(1996).
Annual Report (Penyrenglyn Project). Bridges Community Support
Team. (1999).

CHAPTER 4 – LISTENING TO THE RHYDYFELIN COMMUNITY PROJECT
Adams Dave. Rhydyfelin Community Assessment Needs. University
of Glamorgan (2000).
Ap Nicholas Islwyn. A Welsh Heretic – Dr William Price. Ffynon P.
(1972).
Rhondda Cynon Taf's Community Strategy. Live. Grow. Aspire.
Achieve. (2010 – 2020). www.rctbc.gov.uk
UK Census. Office for National Statistics (2001).
Young Kerry. The Art of Youth Work. Russell House (2006.)

CHAPTER 5 – FINDING OUT ABOUT THE PEN DINAS COMMUNITY PROJECT.
Hughes Katherine. Dinas Feasibility Study. Katherine Hughes
Associates (2003).
Princes Trust Youth Index. (2013).
Report from Valleys Kids Archives:
Cutland Liz and Olney Jo. Through the Eyes of Children. (2003).

CHAPTER 6 - CATCHING UP WITH THE PENYGRAIG COMMUNITY PROJECT
Heritage Trail Sites. The History of Penygraig. Rhondda Cynon Taf
Library Service. www.rhondda-cynon-taff.gov.uk/heritagetrail/english/
rhondda/penygraig/html.

CHAPTER 7 – CAN YOU HEAR ME NOW?
Ballin Miranda. A Study in Youth Arts – An Elucidation of the
Professional Paradigm of the Youth Artsworker. University of
Glamorgan. (2009).
Cunningham Hugh. The Invention of Childhood. BBC Books (2006).
Estyn Report. Sex and Relationships Guidance. Estyn (2007).
European Comission. Joint Report on Social Inclusion. (2002).
Gill Tim. No Fear: Growing Up in a Risk Averse Society. Calouste
Gulbenkian Foundation (2007).
Hirsch Donald. Through Thick and Thin: Tackling Poverty in Hard

Times. Written for End Child Poverty (2009).

Lewis Dr Richard. Are We Failing Our Children? Wales on Line.

Margo and Dixon. Freedom's Orphans: Raising Youth Awareness in a Changing World. Prince Town University Press (2007).

McColl Davina. Lets Talk Sex. Channel Four.

Nichols Michael P. The Lost Art of Listening: How Learning to Listen Can Help Improve Relationships. Guilford Press (2009).

Palmer Sue. Toxic Childhood. Orion (2007).

Save the Children. Child Poverty Solutions - Wales.

Welsh Government – Education for All for the Wellbeing of Children. (2007).

Wood and Hine. Work with Young People: Theory and Policy for Practice. Sage Publications (2009).

Young Kirsty. The British Family. BBC 2. (2010).

Report from Valleys Kids Archives: Hidden Potential. (1996)

CHAPTER 8 – DISCOVERING A VOICE.

Ballin Miranda. A Study in Youth Arts – An Elucidation of the Professional Paradigm of the Youth Artsworker. University of Glamorgan (2009)

National Public Health Service for Wales. Suicide in Wales: Data to Support Implementation of the National Action Plan to Reduce Suicide and Self Harm in Wales. NPHS Wales (2008).

Nichols Michael P. The Lost Art of Listening: How Learning to Listen can Help Improve Relationships. Guilford Press (2009).

Whitfield Charles. Healing the Child Within. Health Communications (1991).

Report from Valleys Kids Archives: Journey Makers - ArtsWorks Business Plan. (2010 – 2013).

CHAPTER 9 – THE SOUNDING BOARD OF FAMILY.

Bevan Foundation. What is poverty? www.bevanfoundation.org. (2010).

Fuller and Taylor. A Toolkit for Motivational Skills. Wiley-Blackwell. (2008).

Hunt Candida. The Parenting Puzzle – How to Get the Best Out of Family Life. The Family Links Nurturing Programme. (2003).

Gerhadt Sue. The Selfish Society. Simon and Schuster (2010).

Wilson and Pickett. The Spirit Level – Why Equality is better for Everyone. Penguin Books (2010).

Reports from Valleys Kids Archives:
Bridges Community Support Scheme Review (2003-2004).
Future Families Project Plan (2010).
Hamme-Hategekimana Kerstin. Participatory Action Research into the Effectiveness of the Feeling Good Groups in the Rhondda Valleys. (2006).

CHAPTER 10 – HEEDING THE TUG OF CURIOSITY
Allan and Edwards. Torchbearers - Fear Will Never Keep Us Apart. A Valleys Kids publication (2012).
Kellner Pringle Mia. The Needs of Children. Routeledge. (Third edition1986).
Save the Children. Giving Children a Chance. (2011).
Reports from Valleys Kids Archives:
10th Newsletter (2004).
Strategic Plan – The Way Ahead (2013 – 2016).
Torchbearers – The Programme (2012).

CHAPTER 11 – AMPLIFYING THE SENSE OF COMMUNITY
Allan and Edwards. Torchbearers – Fear Will Never Keep Us Apart. A Valleys Kids Publication (2012).
Dance for All. Stargaze – 21st Anniversary Gala (2012).
Stengel Richard. Mandela's Way – Lessons in Life. Virgin Books (2010).
McMillan And Chavis. Psychological Sense of Community: Theory. Journal of Community Psychology. Volume 14. (1986).
Van Resburg and Esteve. Once Upon a Circus. Zip Zap Circus (2012).

CHAPTER 12 – THE CHALLENGE OF KEEPING CHANNELS OPEN
Allen and Edwards. Torchbearers - Fear Will Never Keep Us Apart. A Valleys Kids Publication (2012).
Frankel and Bromberger. The Art of Social Enterprise. New Society Publishers (2013).
Wood and Hine. Work with Young People – Theory and Policy for Practice. Sage Publications (2009).
Reports from Valleys Kids Archives:
The Pop Factory – Creative Space for the Valley (2010).
The Way Ahead (2013 – 2016).